THE CASE FOR THE FAITH

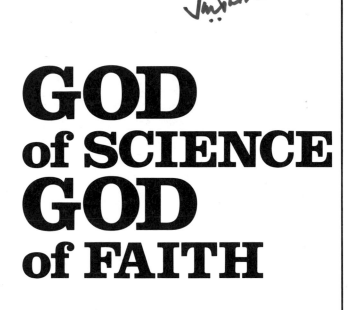

GOD
of SCIENCE
GOD
of FAITH

A Study Guide

Edited by
DAVID BRIDGE

THE METHODIST CHURCH HOME MISSION DIVISION

GOD
of SCIENCE
GOD
of FAITH

First published 1988
Copyright © The Methodist Church Home Mission Division, 1988

ISBN 0-901015-01-6

Printed in Great Britain by
Warners (Midlands) plc, West Street, Bourne, Lincs. PE10 9PH

CONTENTS

PREFACE

IN 1981 THE Methodist Home Mission Division decided to give special attention to apologetics, that is the business of defending the faith against misunderstanding. As we are invited to love God with all our minds, so it should be possible to describe the Christian faith in words in such a way as to require thoughtful people to take it seriously.

Among those who were persuaded to help us in this task were a group of people whose training and profession well qualified them to reflect on matters concerning science and faith. They were asked in particular to look at popular misconceptions of the nature of science and its findings which might prove an obstacle to belief. They were also asked to alert us to anything happening on the frontiers of scientific enquiry which might prove to be a challenge to faith.

This study book is the result. It is published in the hope that individuals and groups will be helped to think more clearly and confidently about the nature of faith in a scientific age. As is usual in collaborative work of this kind the members of the group are identified so that you may have confidence in the book as a whole, but no individual should be held responsible for any particular opinion.

Most of the members of group were professional scientists, but they were glad to welcome and to receive the contributions of some whose primary approach was as ordained ministers. It was at the wish of the group that I acted as chairman and subsequently as editor.

Geoffrey Clark took the lead in preparing the questions for discussion, and to him and all who have given their time and wisdom to this project I am most grateful. In particular I want to thank Geoffrey Gee who has convened the group, persuaded many people to give time to attend it, written many of the more elegant and illuminating passages in the book, and whose gracious personality and intellectual distinction set the tone of the project from beginning to end.

David Bridge

INTRODUCTION

SCIENCE AND RELIGION have often had an uneasy relationship. Eminent scientists have fallen foul of the church. A literal interpretation of the Bible places it at odds with a scientific description of the universe. Some scientists have concluded from their researches that 'God is a hypothesis of which they have no need.' Christians have often felt apprehensive towards scientific enquiry lest it should unearth something which cuts at the root of their faith.

At the same time science has been able to flourish in cultures shaped by the Christian faith. Belief in a benevolent creator encourages the study of creation. Many have seen in the universe's order and design, evidence of a creator's hand. Many distinguished scientists have become or remained believers, declaring that the more they knew about the nature of the universe the more they felt wonder and awe at its intricate unity.

Those who felt it was possible both to affirm science and to affirm God naturally sought for ways to hold the two together and to talk about them sensibly. At one stage it was felt that the best way to do this would be to arrange for a division of territory with God being responsible for certain parts of his universe and science for the rest. It was found however that science could not be confined in this way, and though attempts were made to preserve the principle by moving the boundaries, it soon became clear that the space reserved for God was shrinking to the point of insignificance. An alternative strategy was tried whereby science and religion were admitted to be addressing the same things but from different points of view. Any apparent conflict between them would be resolved once this was recognized, rather like arguing whether a table was square or brown. So science was recognized as more often addressing 'how' questions, whilst religion was more often occupied with 'why' questions.

This was a great advance on the territorial approach and it is not without value even now. It does not help us however to deal with certain basic questions such as 'Is the world, as revealed by science, compatible with the idea of God as consistent and faithful?' 'Is such a world consistent with the ideas of God's sovereignty and redemptive work?' It would indeed be surprising if God created a universe whose nature in no way reflected his own. But if the universe does bear witness to its creator we should expect a study of that universe, of whatever kind, to turn up some of the evidence. Such questions show us the interrelation between science and theology; we cannot put them into different compartments, however sophisticated.

This dilemma becomes particularly acute when we consider the topic of providence. In this book it has a chapter to itself but it can hardly be excluded from any chapter. In what sense can we speak of God as active in creation? How can we speak of God making a difference to people, and perhaps to events, if we cannot study God in a scientific way?

The language we use to describe God and the language we use to describe scientific phenomena will often sound the same. They are not the same but neither are they wholly different. They occupy positions on a line which runs also through the language of poetry, of morality and of aesthetics. At each point there will be an element of the objective, something which can be tested, shared and predicted, but there will also be something else. We have learned that the language of science is not as perfectly objective as was once thought and that the perspective of the observer becomes more important as the scientific enquiry becomes more sophisticated.

The difficulty is to talk about almost anything of consequence without surrounding ourselves with so many qualifications and caveats that we cease to make any sense at all. In fact we usually do it quite well, by using metaphors, images and symbols and all that gives language real quality. We just need to pause from time to time and remind ourselves that this is indeed what we are doing. In this way, although we may make perfect sense of only a few things, we shall make sufficient sense of most things.

In this book we try to make sufficient sense of the world by looking at it both as scientists and Christians. The first two chapters introduce the subject, combining science, poetry and ethics to challenge our traditional way of thinking. Chapter three is in some ways the most important in the whole book. If we understand the ways scientists use language and see the connection between that and the language of faith, we shall avoid much confusion and misunderstanding. In chapter four we begin the story over again and follow the life of the universe from beginning to end. This method involves a small amount of repetition but enables each chapter to be studied without the need for frequent reference elsewhere.

To study the universe as believers in God and in the scientific method is to make a voyage of discovery, not least about ourselves. We invite you to travel with us.

CHAPTER ONE

GENESIS ONE —
A Scientist's Version

Day 1. In the beginning was the Big Bang. It happened about 15 billion (15,000,000,000) years ago. We have no knowledge of anything before that, so time itself can properly be said to start then. Everything that is now in our universe was there, but in a very different form: concentrated into a tiny volume inconceivably dense and hot, and completely chaotic. It was the whole primitive universe, and represented the potential from which today's world (including us) was to develop.

From the instant of the Big Bang, the universe started to expand and cool. By an age of one second the first building blocks of nuclear particles and atoms had appeared in the form of protons with a single positive electric charge, neutrons of similar mass but no charge and (much lighter) electrons with a single negative charge. Within 1,000 seconds a quarter of the protons had combined with an equal number of neutrons to form the nuclei of helium each consisting of 2 protons and 2 neutrons; tiny amounts of deuterium and lithium were also formed. These nuclei including that of hydrogen (the proton) were immersed in a sea of electrons. The major part of the energy in this early universe was in the form of radiation which constantly interacted with the nuclei and electrons. This plasma of radiation and matter was expanding rapidly.

Day 2. After this furious start, some 3 billion years elapsed, during which this universe of hydrogen, helium and radiation continued to expand and cool. The first structure began to appear; local regions of greater density separated out, encouraged by gravitational forces, so that a dense region tended to get denser. By the end of this long period the broad outline of the present astronomical picture was established in the form of two levels of structure, galaxies and stars. The imagination boggles at the numbers involved. The universe we see at present is estimated to contain about 100 billion (100 thousand million) galaxies and on average each of these contains about 100 billion stars; a stupendous total of 10 thousand billion billion stars, or 2 thousand billion for each human being alive today. Stars are still being born, living and dying. They differ among themselves; some burn fiercely in relatively short lives, others are quieter and longer lived. The source of their energy is through nuclear reactions in the hot centres of the stars where mass is lost in exchange for energy. During these long lasting processes, the primary protons, neutrons and electrons interact in complex but well-understood ways to produce the atoms of all the elements we now find on the Earth. The world of a star is violent; not only are energetic nuclear processes occurring at its centre, but it can ultimately shed its outer shell of gas before collapsing to form a cool interstellar cinder. The survivors at any time are mostly stars which like our Sun are relatively stable under their prevailing conditions.

Day 3. We jump another 7 billion years, to a time about 4 billion years ago, when one particular star — our Sun — was formed with a family of planets and other smaller bodies, the asteroids and comets. We are especially interested in the planet which we call Earth and in its moon. There seems every reason to think that vast numbers of stars must have similar planetary systems and that there have been and still are very many planets basically similar to the Earth.

The newborn Earth, though much cooler than the Sun, was still pretty hot by our everyday standards, but too cool to support nuclear reactions, (except for the decay of what we call radioactive elements) and most of its heat now came from the Sun. The Earth eventually cooled to about its present temperature. This lower temperature provided the conditions for the start of a rich chemistry in which atoms combine with one another to form molecules, e.g. one oxygen plus two hydrogens to give a molecule of water. A further level of organisation occurred, in which molecules, or atoms, packed closely together to produce liquids and solids. Iron, the most abundant dense element settled under gravity at the centre of the Earth; under the immense prevailing pressures this iron became the liquid core of the Earth. Floating on the iron core was rocky material consisting of a complex mixture of substances formed out of the chemical compounds which proved stable. To begin with there was no liquid water — only steam forming part of an atmosphere very different from that of today. When the temperature fell low enough for steam to condense there must have occurred stupendous rainstorms, leading to erosion of the rocks and the appearance of the primitive seas and lakes. It must have been a desolate landscape of rocks and water disturbed by frequent storms, earthquakes, and volcanic eruptions, with an atmosphere made up principally of the very simple molecules hydrogen, carbon monoxide, ammonia and methane — none of them capable of supporting life as we now know it. More complex molecules were present in solution in the water. And so the Earth was formed.

Day 4. It was another billion years before life appeared in any recognisable form. During that period the initial molecules had interacted (in ways which have been to some extent imitated in the laboratory) to produce a whole range of new chemical compounds. Prominent among them were sugars, amino acids and nucleic acids, which had the important property of being able to join up (polymerize) to produce eventually huge molecules, including those which we know as proteins. Initially these chemical reactions must have been completely random, depending on chance collisions between molecules, and it is not entirely clear how from these beginnings there developed the precisely controlled system of molecular growth seen in living things. Possibly some of the solid surfaces in the rocks provided templates for the early stages. What is clear is that over this very extended period processes became established, by which complex molecules were routinely built up from small ones. These processes have been elucidated in the laboratory only in the last few years. They involve the compounds usually referred to as DNA and RNA (see page 53). Molecules of RNA and DNA react with various simpler compounds in two main ways. In one of these types of reaction they produce more molecules like themselves. In the other they produce protein molecules, of which it is currently estimated that as many as a million different kinds are to be found in nature. These reactions, and others which some of the protein molecules themselves bring about, form the chemical basis of life.

The earliest forms of life certainly appeared in the water and are believed to have been bacteria-like, probably no more than 1/100 millimetre across — tiny but still huge compared with the largest molecule. These bacteria 'learned' to use the Sun's energy to help them synthesize the food they needed for growth from the simpler compounds in their environment. This is 'life' at its most primitive, and bacteria have, from this early stage right up to today, proved extraordinarily adaptable in making use of whatever raw material is available, succeeding under what might seem impossibly adverse conditions. Other very simple early arrivals were algae, now known simply as 'blue-greens', which 'discovered' how to extract hydrogen from water. This was a vital step in the Earth's history, for it liberated oxygen and so very gradually changed the composition of the atmosphere towards that which we now breathe.

Day 5. There was still much to be done before vegetation and animal life could begin to appear. Plants and trees need structural materials; animals need highly specialised systems of internal organisation, movement and interaction with the environment. It is not possible to give a detailed account of the diverse ways in which these needs were met but it is believed that the general method might be described as one of progressive experiment, of trial and error. From any given point of development, possible ways forward were explored; unsuccessful ones simply disappeared; successful ones led on — and on. The process works because the number of individuals involved is enormous. The end product (if there is an 'end') is not necessarily unique, for example different creatures learning how to see have not all produced the same kind of eye.

The conquest of the land by plants and animals was difficult because of the universal need for water. It is only some 500 million years since the first land plants appeared while flowering plants have only developed in the last 100 million years. Different lines of development led to the appearance of the rich variety of species we recognise today. The fossil record shows fishes 450 million years ago, insects and amphibians 350, reptiles 300, mammals 200 and birds 150. A fascinating account of the appearance of the various species is to be found in David Attenborough's book *Life on Earth*. One of the success stories is that of the insects. Some 700,000 different species have been described and named, and there are probably several times this number awaiting identification. A rough estimate of the total number of individual insects alive at any moment suggests that it may well be a million times the world population of human beings. The reason is that insects are small in relation to the features of their environment. There are many more ways of making a living as an insect than as a mammal. We are led to imagine again a process of random experimentation, with rejection of failures and growth by selection of successful features. This method of natural selection is believed to be very general and to provide the key to understanding the way in which species develop in response to a need. Consider as an example the different ways in which creatures find their way about. Most have eyes, though not all eyes are alike. Some use a form of echo sounding, in which they emit a sound and listen for the echo. Some birds are believed to make use of the Earth's magnetic field in migrating over long distances. Some fishes create and respond to electric fields. The diversity of the living world is immense, our understanding of it limited and of very recent growth.

Day 6. The appearance of mammals about 200 million years ago brings us almost up to date. Their immediate predecessors were a group of reptiles which were numerous and highly successful in the period from 280 to 200 million years ago. During the period from 200 million to 65 million years ago another group of reptiles — the dinosaurs — held centre-stage, and the mammals remained small and inconspicuous. Then suddenly (by geological standards) the fossil record shows the total elimination of creatures such as dinosaurs, and over the next few million years the first large mammals appeared. It is believed by some that the disappearance of the dinosaurs was the result of a catastrophic event — possibly the impact of a large meteorite. There have certainly been other catastrophes of this kind though of varying magnitudes. Apart from such rare events the history of living creatures records many failures; species arise, live and reproduce for a time (a million years is not long in the history of the universe) and disappear. It has been estimated that of all the animal species that ever existed, only one per cent is alive now. So ultimate extinction is both the rule and the price of progress.

The story of the appearance of human beings is well told in Richard E. Leakey's book *The Making of Mankind.* Dating man's first appearance depends on agreeing a definition of 'man', for the fossil evidence shows us arising from ape-like ancestors. Modern man is called *Homo sapiens* and first appeared some 100,000 years ago; the immediate forbears *(Homo erectus)* 1 to 2 million years ago. We have been fruitful and have multiplied. 10,000 years ago human beings probably totalled about 10 millions, 2,000 years ago it was 300 millions and subsequent growth has been dramatic, now exceeding 5,000 millions. We have become the most numerous among large animals. In many ways we are typical animals and our origin and early development are certainly to be understood on the same general principles of natural selection that operate throughout the living world.

Day 7. According to Genesis 2, God rested on the seventh day. The job was done, everything was created, and leisure also is declared to be part of God's creative purpose. The scientist's picture is very different; creation is a continuing process, stars form and die, species come and go. In describing it we have not spoken of God, of plan or of purpose. The scientist who believes in God must see the picture he draws of creation as evidence of the way in which God works. The scientist, speaking only in his professional capacity, cannot comment on the ultimate purposes of God. For this he must turn, with his fellow believers, to the insights of religion.

Questions for Discussion

1. Read Genesis 1 in the Bible. In what ways is it similar to this chapter and in what ways different?

2. 'The scientist . . . . . . cannot comment on the ultimate purposes of God.' Why not?

3. Is it helpful to try and match a modern scientist's understanding of creation with that of a religious writer many thousands of years ago? How does the comparison enrich your picture of God?

How does it alter your perception of the Bible?

4.   There appear to be different accounts of the origins of human life. In Genesis man and woman are created by God's special act, whereas scientists speak of human beings evolving as part of the created order. Are these real differences, and what are the implications for understanding our relationship with God and with the rest of creation?

CHAPTER TWO

MAN TAKES A HAND

IN THIS CHAPTER we look at some of the ways in which the course of evolution has been changed by the development of the human species.

The fossil record of human origins is admittedly much less extensive than could be wished. In the absence of complete skeletons the structure of our early ancestors has been deduced from incomplete sets of bones found at sites in various parts of the world. The precise conclusions to be drawn have been the subject of much argument among experts, but it is now believed that not all the types identified can be fitted into a single line. Rather it would seem that the evolution of what are collectively termed 'hominids' made a number of starts, most of which ended in extinction, before the line leading to modern man became established.

Before the arrival of the human species, plants, fishes, insects, birds and animals lived together in a state of mutual interdependence. The rotating seasons would bring their regular pattern, and on the time scale of a century little overall change would be apparent, though there would certainly be local fluctuations from year to year. Over longer times the alternation of ice ages with warmer periods would result in more extensive changes. Evolutionary change would be evident only on a still longer time scale. We might express this by saying that the different elements in the universe had 'learned' to live together, competing yet in a dynamic equilibrium. The phrase 'nature red in tooth and claw' emphasises the fact that some animals can only survive by using others for food, but we must also remember that different species are frequently interdependent.

Into this world came human beings and a totally new element was introduced. For the first time there was a creature which could deliberately interfere with nature.

It began modestly. Early men and women developed skills in hunting and in finding food from plants but their numbers were small, both in total and in the size of local groups, and their immediate influence on the world would seem negligible. It grew with the start of settled agriculture some 10,000 years ago by which time the human population had reached about 10 millions and larger communities were developing. Agriculture led to the clearance of forests, cultivation of the ground, and the beginnings of plant and animal breeding. This is a highly significant landmark in our history for here we see people taking advantage of the variations which make evolution possible, but introducing a bias by their own deliberate choice. They decide what is to grow, what rejected. A flower, which had developed its form and colour to attract insects to transfer pollen and so secure its own propagation, is modified by selection to produce a form pleasing to the human eye. Population growth and the need for tools and energy required for large scale cultivation have stimulated the developments apparent in modern agriculture. We have taken pride in our achievements but we have also made mistakes, some of which are only just beginning to be widely acknowledged. A parallel story concerns our exploitation of limited mineral resources, e.g. of coal and oil. Our treatment of animals presents additional grounds for concern; species are threatened not only by our destruction of their environment, but by slaughter for food, for other uses, or simply in the name of sport. Many of these problems have arisen in part because of the new powers we have required through the application of science. It does not necessarily follow that the blame should be laid at the door of the scientist.

For most of the 10,000 or so years which have elapsed since the beginning of settled agriculture and the development of the first cities, science has influenced human society in many ways. It has changed the style of our buildings, enhanced our ability to exploit natural resources, affected warfare, travel, and the nature of work. Its importance during this period however was not as great as that of other factors such as economics, family and tribal relationships, religion, philosophy and politics. This situation has changed dramatically during the present century when the discoveries of science, and even more their practical application, have given us the power to shape our destinies in ways undreamed of by former generations.

Until very recently the public perception of science has focussed on spectacular achievements in the physical world, especially space flight and the harnessing of nuclear energy for both peace and war. Science has been alternately praised for perceived benefits and blamed for accidents and potential disasters. The threats are real enough; for the first time mankind possesses the ability to create destruction on a scale which would leave little of our present world intact. The science which has posed these awesome problems has arisen naturally as a consequence of our insatiable urge to understand the world. The problems are moral and political, and the professional responsibility of the scientist is to ensure that the problems are fully and accurately represented so that all can share in making the political judgements and taking the necessary action. Many would argue that while it would be wrong to curtail basic science, it would be proper to limit work on, say, weapon development, or to seek new energy sources other than nuclear.

Even more remarkable than our conquest of the physical world is what may be called the molecular revolution, which has taken us very close to the understanding and control of life itself. To see how this has arisen we should begin by recalling what chemistry is about. It is concerned essentially with the study of the ways in which atoms (created initially in the stars) combine together to form structures we call molecules; which in turn can interact by transferring groups of atoms from one to another. Much of life as we know it can be described in these terms, the fire we burn to keep us warm, the food we eat to give us energy. Our bodies can be thought of as factories in which complex chemistry is continually occurring, creating electric currents which flow along our nerves and stimulating mechanical action to move our various organs. Elucidation of these processes has only become possible as a result of major advances in laboratory chemistry. For many years an important branch of this subject has been concerned with extracting chemical compounds from plants, determining their molecular make-up and trying to devise ways of creating (synthesising) them in the laboratory from simple starting materials. This work has branched out in three ways, as scientists have asked;

— How does nature make these compounds?

— Can we make them in the laboratory?

— Can we make other compounds, not formed in nature, which are more or less similar to natural ones?

The answers to the second and third of these have often been yes. This has led to the founding of the fibres industry which has given us nylon, rayon and terylene to set alongside silk, cotton and wool; and the development of the pharmaceuticals industry with its wide range of products. The first question has proved harder, but a general answer is now possible. It turns out that nature has developed a very powerful technique for controlling the formation of the protein molecules which occupy a central role in all living material, plant, animal and human. The key is found in the molecules DNA and RNA (to which reference is made on page 53), which store and pass on the instructions needed to ensure that the required structure is produced. Their reliability is shown by the high degree of success observed in natural reproduction. But chance still plays a part and is shown here in the occurrence of mistakes; sometimes the protein produced is not exactly right. When this happens we observe the effect in some defect of the living material. The most recent developments arise from the realisation that if we could get at the controlling DNA and RNA it would be possible in principle to change the instructions, and this has indeed been done in some simple cases. We need molecular 'scissors' to snip a bit from one molecule and insert it into another. By doing this, certain bacteria have been induced to make insulin, otherwise only available (with difficulty) from animal sources. In the same way plants can be modified, not by selection, but by changing their programmes. The potential of this kind of work appears immense.

These remarkable achievements cause us to rethink some of our attitudes to human life. Sickness was treated by empirical concoctions from natural products long before we had any idea what the active agent was. We now understand much better the causes of sickness and can deploy a range of well-defined substances as remedies. We begin to understand what has gone wrong at the molecular level to cause physical and mental handicaps. Our understanding might be deepened by studying the embryo which already contains the controlling DNA. That serious ethical problems are raised by research on human embryos, hardly needs to be stated.

Can scientists and theologians collaborate in seeking solutions to such problems? The early chapters of the book of Genesis contain both scientific and theological insights. They speak of the order and dependability of the natural world. They describe creation as a progression of events in which mankind, albeit a special order of creation, is a late arrival on the scene. They make clear where responsibility lies, with God but shared by him with all mankind. Human beings are to have dominion over all that God has made, but that does not mean they can do with it as they like. In the story of the Garden of Eden we see a man and a woman misusing the natural world with the result that the dynamic equilibrium is lost.

There is no way back to paradise, the way is barred by an angel with a flaming sword. The only possibility is to go forward in search of a new way for mankind to live with the rest of creation. It is as futile to deplore the advance of scientific knowledge as it is to long for the lost innocence of childhood. The question that matters is; can we harness the insights of both science and faith before it is too late?

Questions for Discussion

1. We are made in the image of God, says the writer of Genesis. 'The Earth is the Lord's and the fulness thereof, the world and those who dwell in it', sings the Psalmist. What do such phrases

say about our rights and responsibilities as part of the created order?

2.   Is science too important to be left to the scientists? What ethical and theological criteria, if any, should be used to regulate scientific research?

3.   In the Genesis story, God gives human beings dominion over the rest of creation. Does this mean we can use it as we please? Or are there other biblical truths which indicate how we should use the natural world? If so, what are they? How should they influence our attitudes to such contemporary issues as nuclear power, environmental pollution, and the consumption of fossil fuels?

4.   During the present century the ability of the human race to affect the environment has increased immeasurably. People have felt liberated by the resources of science and technology, and the phrase 'playing God' has been used to describe the situation of those who have this new power. How should this influence the way we think about God?

CHAPTER THREE

SCIENCE AND THE USE OF MODELS

IN THE 1950s science was widely seen as the great hope of mankind, though what was judged so exciting was rather the technology made possible by the application of science. This was soon followed by the realisation that technology could produce new problems and new dangers as well as new achievements. The sight of the victims of radiation released through atomic explosions, the effects on our environment of pollution and the excessive exploitation of natural resources, the ethical implications of new advances in medical science, all caused people to wonder if science should not be regarded as devilish rather than divine. It is of course neither. In this chapter we shall emphasise its essential nature — to observe, measure and describe the world, and to seek explanations for what is found. Measurement is important. We feel confident when we can put a number on something and more confident when we can suggest a reason for that number. In its simplest form science is restricted to things and events which we can appreciate directly with our senses, not too large or too small, not too fast or too slow. We extend this range by making use of a growing range of instruments to help us. As an example of science at work we might mention an area of study encountered by virtually all science students under the somewhat forbidding title of thermodynamics. It crops up in all sorts of ways. One of its origins was the study of steam engines; this led to the recognition of limits on the efficiency with which the energy in the fuel could be used to perform useful work. Another example is the measurement of the way in which pressure, volume and temperature are related, the 'gas laws' of school physics. Having made measurements such as these, there are three questions to be asked:

— Can we find a mathematical formula which summarises our results?

— Can we find a relationship between the results of two or more kinds of measurement?

— Can we understand in a more fundamental way what is going on?

In the world of thermodynamics the answer to all three is yes.

Matter at the molecular level

Success in answering the first two questions has been so widespread that it has led to a view of the world described as deterministic. This means that if we can describe something in sufficient detail, and if we also know what is happening to it now, we should in principle be able to predict its future exactly. By a sweeping extension of this argument to human affairs some have argued that it gets rid of any need for God and leaves no room for free will or individual responsibility. But it now seems that nature is not at heart deterministic, but that the laws of probability play an important role. We can get an idea of how this works by thinking about the interpretation of the gas laws mentioned above. The volume of any gas on which measurements are made contains an enormous number of molecules in motion; for example in one litre of air at normal pressure there are approximately 3×10^{22} (thirty thousand million million million) molecules, a figure, it will be noted, which is similar to that for the number of stars in the universe. If we think of each molecule as a very tiny ball, then we say that the pressure they exert arises from the collisions taking place in this swarm of balls, three-dimensional snooker on a vast scale. The deterministic view would be that if we could once locate all these balls and their movements we could predict their future. Modern physics says this is impossible, there is no way in which we can measure simultaneously and accurately both the position and the movement of even a single molecule. All we can talk about is the probability that any molecule will have certain properties. What we observe is the average behaviour and because the numbers involved are so huge the average can be very accurately known, even when we know next to nothing about any individual molecule. So nature's laws can be — and often are — exceedingly reliable when applied to the sort of quantities we can see and handle, but subject to different rules when we try to study the individual.

We have chosen a very simple example to introduce the idea that the world we find when we get down to the molecular level looks very different from our everyday world. This is important in our attempts to understand any natural phenomenon or observation for it is often necessary to get down to the behaviour of molecules — a world of very small distances and exceedingly brief times. When we enter this new world we encounter other surprises. In particular we begin to observe 'quantum' behaviour, i.e. quantities such as light and energy which had always seemed to be available in any sort of quantity now turn up only in integral packets; you can have 1, 2, 3, 4 but not 1.1, 2.1, 3.1, 4.1, ... etc. The reason for our surprise at these new discoveries is that we had, consciously or not, assumed that everything we knew about our everyday world could be applied universally, simply by altering the scale. It is now clear that this natural but naive assumption is wrong. We have to recognise the laws of small systems as fundamental and our everyday laws as approximations which work well simply because our everyday world is so large, for they do work well and the engineer has not had to rewrite his text books.

Scientific models
Another kind of difficulty arises when we try to describe this sub-sub-microscopic world. The mathematician may be satisfied with a series of equations, but most of us need some kind of picture or model as an extra prop. The difficulty is that we can only describe something new by making use of what is already familiar. If we simply invent a new name it may be useful as a label but it tells us nothing. We describe our everyday world by a series of convenient similes, e.g. we describe a person as being 'as thin as a rake', we speak of something being squashed 'as flat as a pancake'. These descriptions succeed because the hearer can immediately translate them into pictures. In the development of our understanding of the structure of matter the

first step was the recognition of the atom as the ultimate unit of any chemical element. It was thought of as indivisible, and a molecule was envisaged as a three-dimensional structure made up by linking atoms together with 'bonds'. The simplest way to model this description is to use different kinds of balls to represent different atoms and to provide rods of different lengths and strengths to join them together. We now know that atoms are themselves complex, so that a ball is only a very crude model. Additional evidence leads to the modelling of an atom as a small solar system with electrons orbiting around a nucleus, tiny even in comparison with the atom, though this model is still very crude and has been replaced by an electron cloud model. Today high energy physics probes the interior of the nucleus in search of even smaller scale structure. With all this complexity to cope with, the total description of even the simplest chemical compound begins to look like an impossible task. Fortunately for most purposes it is a task which need not be attempted. The scientist regularly uses quite crude models as an aid not simply to providing a picture but as a basis for useful and valid calculations. In discussing the gas laws we modelled a molecule as a ball. The next step on is to use a ball and rod model.

The use of models then is very widespread in science but, being human, individual scientists have not always recognised the limitations of models as factual descriptions. This failure is very well illustrated by the controversy regarding the nature of light. The evidence was confusing; some experiments suggested that light consists of particles, others that it was a wave motion. The argument assumed that one or other must be wrong. We now realise that it is meaningless to ask which of these models is true. What we have to say is that in some experiments light behaves in a way which we associate with particles we can see and handle, while in other experiments its behaviour reminds us of waves on a pond. The two models are not to be seen as contradictory; together they tell us more than either does separately. In the course of time, quantum electrodynamics has enabled us to replace these two inadequate models by something more satisfactory.

In summary, our picture of science is of a continuous probing into the nature of our world. Our examples have been drawn from the physical world, but science recognises neither division nor limitations. There are no set boundaries at which we are write finis, Q.E.D., or other signing off symbols. The challenge to understand is unceasing, but at any particular time science can offer a description (to be continuously updated) of the world as revealed in observation and experiment, and can suggest theoretical interpretations of whatever has been seen. In all this models have a very valuable role to play, they are not alternatives to truth but approximations to it and pointers towards a fuller truth.

Theological models

At first sight the religious view of the world is totally different and most discussions of the relationship between the two have tacitly assumed this to be inevitable. We believe, on the contrary, that the two approaches are complementary rather than mutually exclusive, and that much is to be gained by encouraging their interaction. One type of approach, often favoured, we find particularly unhelpful. This seeks to share the world between religion and science with a boundary which is thought of as rigid, even though its location has not always been the same. The outcome of such thinking is in effect to look to science to explain what it can and to call on God for the rest. This 'God of the gaps' model diminishes both science and theology by attempting to set limits to their relevance to our experience of the world. Neither science nor theology take kindly to a *Keep Out* sign.

We find a common approach in the concept of models. Any religion must face the task of finding words to describe whatever is conceived to lie at the heart and centre of our world. The problem echoes in even more acute form that of the scientist seeking to describe something which cannot be directly perceived. Primitive religions have spoken of spirits related to the giant forces of nature, but the Christian faith in common with many other world religions looks towards one Supreme Being. Though we are unable to know fully the nature of this Being, we call him God and attribute to him the quality of personality. We have in so doing constructed our first and most elementary religious model. The choice is natural, God must be greater than ourselves and we know of nothing in nature which could be preferred to our personhood as our basic model. Of course it is too crude to be completely satisfactory and the task of theology could be seen as that of refining the model. How is this to be done? The scientist observes and experiments. The theologian's place of work is the world and part of his task is the study of human attempts to communicate with God. The material available is the whole of religious experience especially as recorded in the Bible, in the history of the church to the present day and, not least, in our own lives. Whatever may be the shortcomings of the words in which our faith is expressed the experience affords valid evidence which should be taken seriously, even though it is often hard in practice to separate it from the intellectual framework we construct around it.

Some people see in the Old Testament a God who conforms to a simple model. He creates and rules the world, communicates with his chosen people, instructs, approves, reprimands, punishes. The model undergoes development in the teaching of successive prophets, but it remains a model. In the Old Testament, to see God face to face or to speak his name is an act of the utmost presumption. Then Jesus comes and asserts that 'He that hath seen me hath seen the Father' which gives us a new and more powerful way of visualizing God. When we speak of Jesus as Son of God we make use of one of the most intimate human relationships to create another model, not replacing but supplementing the first. And when we speak of the Holy Spirit as God we have added a third model. The concept of the Trinity, embodying the three different models of Father, Son and Holy Spirit, is strikingly parallel to the scientist's combination of such seemingly irreconcilable models as particle and wave. 'God in three persons' is a richer concept than any of its parts.

So far we have spoken of scientific models as a way of providing us with something that can be grasped by the mind. The relevance of this to theology is clear. However scientific models have another purpose which is to provide something which can be experimentally tested. Is there a way in which this too applies to theology? Or are theological statements forever protected from having to show themselves true or false? Indeed they are not. Theological statements positively invite us to verify their claims, in the words of the Psalmist to 'taste and see how gracious the Lord is'. Scientists test models by seeing if they are consistent with the available evidence. Statements about God are also models which may be tested in our experience. They are metaphors, but we are entitled to ask if they are metaphors of truth or falsehood.

Theology has no special privileges, it can take its chance in the real world where questions of truth and untruth matter.

In the chapters that follow we shall look at a variety of topics which raise both scientific and theological questions. In the light of this discussion of models and metaphors we shall ask what the answers are and whether it is possible to believe them.

Questions for Discussion

1. To call Jesus 'Son of God' is to use a model to help us understand something about him. Is it helpful to think of the other statements about Jesus in the Apostles' Creed as models?

2. The models we choose to describe God reflect our culture. What models in current use are more of a hindrance than a help because they belong to a culture which has passed?

3. How can the models used by believers when they speak about God be tested as scientists' models are tested?

4. The chapter argues against the view that if two views disagree, one of them must necessarily be wrong. Can you think of other illustrations of this from everyday life, e.g. world maps according to different projections, or photographs of the same scene taken with different cameras?

CHAPTER FOUR

CREATION

SCIENCE AND RELIGION have most frequently been seen to be at odds over matters concerning the creation of the universe. It is claimed that science has disproved the account of creation given in the early chapters of Genesis, thereby undermining the very foundations of religion. In reply some Christians have sought to separate entirely scientific and religious descriptions of the universe including creation. Others, taking the approach commended in this book, see God as working through the creative process. This approach can have its dangers too, for it may lead the Christian to prefer those scientific accounts of creation which seem to reflect a particular theological view, rather than those which give the best explanation of the available evidence. In this way some welcomed the continuous creation theory of Professor Fred Hoyle because it seemed appropriate that God's creative activity should have no beginning and no end, for God was eternal. This theory now finds little support; new evidence strongly favours the view of a universe which is evolving from a Big Bang located precisely in time.

In this chapter we offer an account of how scientists describe and account for some of the great creative processes which have led to the world we see around us. We also look at theological issues raised by this scientific enquiry, and seek ways in which a common scientific and theological view of creation might be derived. The chapter concludes with a discussion of some of these questions from the standpoint of scientists and theologians working as partners rather than antagonists.

Our place in creation
We are inextricably tied in with the whole of creation. Our very

existence is a parable of creation. The fabric of our bodies, the basic elements of carbon, nitrogen, oxygen and all the heavier elements, were formed in generations of stars which were born and died more than 5 billion years ago. These elements then came together under the all-pervading force of gravity to form the Sun and the planets, including our own Earth. We are made of this Earth-material which binds us to the rest of the animal kingdom and to the plant kingdom. Moreover we depend upon animals and plants to sustain our lives. The processes which have ultimately led to the emergence of humankind on Earth are the rightful study of the modern scientist.

The study of creation

In scientific terms, creation is a process which began some 15 billion years ago, is continuing today and will go on into the future as long as matter exists. Although we stress this continuity, there have been pivotal events in the flow of time which have led to the emergence of the Earth and its people. The crucial event which triggered the whole creative process was the so-called Big Bang at the beginning of time. This was followed in due course by the formation of the galaxies, the stars and their encircling planets, the emergence of life on Earth, the catastrophic events which produced the great extinctions of life forms such as the dinosaurs 65 million years ago, and ultimately the appearance of men and women. A broad range of scientific disciplines has contributed to this study of creation; they include the physics and astronomy of the Big Bang, the galaxies and stars, the mathematics of space-time and cosmology, the chemistry of the interstellar gas and chemical processes on Earth, together with the geology and biology of the emergence of life and its environment on Earth.

A physical description of the origins of the universe

In general we shall confine ourselves to that which is commonly agreed among scientists, though noting that there are some areas of uncertainty and disagreement which are matters of continuing research.

Our universe began as an incredibly dense mass, no bigger than a human hand, with all the matter and radiation which now exists. It was very hot and very dense and expanded with great rapidity; this phenomenon is the Big Bang. The first few moments of creation have become of intense interest to scientists in recent years. Investigations of these initial seconds of the creative process may provide answers to fundamental questions in physics, questions about why things are as they are. Events or properties of the universe which once looked random or arbitrary may now be seen to have an explanation. We have already noted in Chapter 1 that about a quarter of the atoms in the universe are helium, an observed fact that had no explanation before the Big Bang was identified.

What has led scientists to describe creation in terms of a massive explosion from a single point? Two major discoveries during this century have pointed in this direction. The first was Edwin Hubble's discovery in 1928 that the universe was expanding, that the galaxies were becoming further apart from each other with a speed that was proportional to their distance. This result implied that the universe was expanding from a more dense phase. The second discovery was by Arno Penzias and Robert Wilson in 1965 who detected evidence of the afterglow of the fireball which accompanied the Big Bang. This radiation field, like the galaxies, has been expanding into space, becoming less dense and cooling with passing time. It was a crucial component of the early universe and dominated its energy content. These two fundamental discoveries and many others during this century, provide an unequivocal picture of an expanding universe evolving from its more compact, higher density origins.

Within the first 1,000 seconds after the Big Bang, hydrogen and helium were formed with traces of deuterium and lithium. Over the subsequent 3 billion years or so, clouds of this gas condensed under the influence of gravity to form the first galaxies studded with stars. Eventually some 100 billion galaxies came into being spanning a range of shapes and sizes. Some are great rotating spirals actively producing stars right up to the present, others formed early into elliptical clouds of stars which are now extremely old. Our own galaxy, the Milky Way, is a large spiral in a group of 20 or so galaxies known as the Local Group.

The continuing process of creation

Within each galaxy stars are continuing to condense out of the primordial gas and then to pass through their own evolutionary cycle. Astronomers have identified stars in the process of birth in our own part of the Milky Way in the constellation of Orion, in Orion's sword. Large stars are intensely bright and live only for a few million years, short on the timescale of the life of a galaxy. Less massive stars are fainter and can shine for billions of years; our own Sun is such a star. Accordingly a spiral galaxy like the Milky Way contains stars with a wide range of ages, brightness and colour, all moving in near-circular orbits about the centre.

As they progress from birth to death, stars perform a crucial role as far as our human existence on Earth is concerned. Deep in their interiors where temperatures are 100 million degrees, the nuclei of all the chemical elements are produced. This process of nucleosynthesis is an integral part of the generation of the nuclear energy which produces the light and heat from the stars. When stars eventually exhaust their nuclear fuel they shed these chemical elements into interstellar space where they mix with the primeval hydrogen and helium from the Big Bang and supply the material from which second generation stars can condense. Our Sun, the Earth and the other planets formed some four and a half billion years ago from this second generation material enriched with all the known elements. The Earth was thereby endowed with the potential for life.

Between one and two billion years after the formation of our planetary system which includes the Sun, the Earth and the Moon, the first microscopic life forms emerged on Earth from this rich chemical environment. The great life forms of the fossil record emerged later again — some 500 million years ago. An increasingly diverse pattern of animal and plant life has continued to appear right up to the present time. Early man *Homo erectus* was a later arrival just two million years ago. While this drama of life was being enacted on Earth, similar dramas were most likely occurring elsewhere in the Milky Way and other galaxies deep in space. Certainly stars like our Sun are commonplace and it is probable that planetary systems are also. It is very unlikely that the Earth is the only planet in the universe which is the home of life.

Though the Big Bang is a kind of beginning, creation is seen to be more than some initial event, it is fundamentally a continuing process. Birth and death are woven into its fabric. New stars are born whilst others are dying; new planets are forming around these new stars. The cycle of animal and plant life continues on Earth. Individuals are born and die, whole species emerge and eventually die out. However, there is now a major new factor at work on Earth. Creatures — humans — have emerged which have the power to control the evolution of life. This is an awesome power, for by its use either accidental or intended, all life that has gone before can be destroyed. In a relatively short time humans have acquired the means of influencing the future for themselves and the rest of creation. They can make the world a garden of Eden or a useless wilderness. There have been no previous creatures with this potential.

Limitations to our experience of creation

One of the major constraints on our experience of creation is imposed by the nature of time itself. The flow of time is only too evident to us all. We conventionally measure its passing by the ticking of our clocks, or more fundamentally by the rotation of the Earth or the oscillations of the caesium atom. We measure the results of the flow of time by the changes that occur in the world around us, on the smallest to the largest scales. This flow is in one direction. There is no turning back — what is past is past. Standing here and now we cannot directly experience or relive what has happened on the Earth in the past; for example we cannot re-observe the Battle of Hastings. However, although cut off from direct experience of the past, we can apply our deductive powers to the records or the archaeological evidence to reconstruct the probable course of events during recent millenia. We can unravel the sequence and timescale of the Earth's crust and the evolution of plant and animal life by the disciplined application of geophysics, geology, palaeontology and cognate sciences. Such studies give us vital clues about the sequence of events which have led to the present, although inevitably much of the Earth's history is lost from the record or has yet to be interpreted.

This onward flow of time however can be put to good use by the astronomer in searching back into the past of objects at great distances from us — in the Milky Way or deep in the universe. This derives from the nature of space-time; space and time are linked in a fundamental way which depends upon the fact that light travels at a finite speed of 300,000 km per second. All astronomical investigations involve the reception of electromagnetic waves in their various forms, light, radio, X-rays, etc. Thus when we look at the Sun we see it as it was 8 minutes ago, or the stars forming in Orion 1,200 years ago, or the Andromeda nebula, our companion galaxy, 2 million years ago, or the most distant galaxies hosting the quasars 10 billion years ago. We can piece together a time-lapse picture of events over almost the whole history of the universe. In reaching back in time however, the astronomer hits a frustrating barrier corresponding to a time when the universe was about a million years old, and cannot observe the Big Bang directly since the radiation was heavily scattered and absorbed before that time. Nevertheless, important and fundamental inferences about the conditions in the Big Bang can be deduced because events and processes at that time have consequences which extend down to the present day.

There are other more obvious limitations to our search for the facts about the creation process. Many of the events or phenomena are so faint, distant or rare that they are at the limit of detection, if detectable at all, with the tools at present available to us. Another possible uncertainty relates to the question of whether the laws of science were the same in the early epochs of the universe as they are now — for example, are the law of gravity and the laws of nuclear physics the same in the Big Bang, in the centre of a star and in a modern Earth-bound laboratory? All evidence appears to suggest that the answer is yes, although there is always some room for doubt. Finally, as for all science, our understanding continues to unfold; new phenomena and laws remain to be discovered. All these limitations notwithstanding, the basic outline of the sequence and processes of creation given in this chapter are considered to be fundamentally correct.

A theological perspective on creation
Is there a religious way of regarding the account of creation just given?

In the Introduction we expressed dissatisfaction with attempts to separate science wholly from theology, whether this was done on the basis of territory or perspective. The book of Genesis claims 'God created ......'. Again and again the biblical writers declare God's responsibility for his creation and his involvement within it. 'The Earth is the Lord's and the fulness thereof.' 'The heavens declare the glory of God and the firmament showeth his handiwork.' However we cannot simply read about God in the pages of the universe because other influences have left their mark. Humans to whom God has given a free will have taken a hand and greed, selfishness and sheer stupidity have taken their part in shaping our world. Nevertheless we recognize in creation the hand of the creator. Writing about the Word, the first principle, which became flesh and dwelt among us, John says 'Through him all things came to be, no single thing was created without him. All that came to be was alive with his life.' The Christian believes that the fullest way of understanding God in his creation is to know Jesus both as a historical figure and as a living Lord and Saviour fully immersed in his creation. St. Paul uses the metaphor 'Creation groaning in travail' to describe the universe as it struggles to give birth to what is new, and at the heart of all this is the Spirit of God. This parallels the message of the cross.

Creation from nothing

When we use the word creation about God's activity we usually imagine him bringing something into existence where previously there was nothing. Yet in every other context we do not use the word creation like this. We speak of the creations of a dress designer or a sculptor and we do not mean they made something out of nothing, rather that out of existing raw materials they made something of their own. The idea of creation out of nothing is difficult for scientists for their investigations reveal a world in which something can be changed into something else, especially matter into energy and vice versa, but never nothing into something. The Big Bang theory of creation holds that everything was present in the dense point from which the universe began. How then did this point come into being? We have no way of answering such a question as matter and energy are, in their various forms, everlasting. At first the idea of matter/energy having no beginning seems contrary to religious belief, yet the alternative is to hold that God was not always a creator. Belief in a God whose essential nature does not change is at the heart of Christianity. It may be that here both science and religion are pointing in the same direction.

Order and design

What inferences should be drawn from the fact that the universe is not only a place of chaos but also of pattern and order, where the various elements relate to each other in ways that are consistent and capable of being observed and formulated? In particular what should we conclude from the fact that of all the possible ways in which the component parts might have come together, they in fact came together in such a way as to allow the emergence of life and eventually of human beings? Are these matters of pure chance, or are they evidence of a guiding spirit behind the structure of the universe? Until recently there has been a tendency to discount this so-called argument from design for the existence of God, but of late many scientists, faced with the amazing number of universes which are theoretically possible, have questioned whether the nature of the universe we have can be accounted for purely by chance. These questions have led some to formulate the Anthropic Principle as a clue to understanding our universe. While few would want to argue that the patterns discovered by scientific enquiry amount to proof of the existence of God, it is recognised that an orderly universe is compatible with the nature of God revealed in Jesus Christ.

The Anthropic Principle

When considering the whole complex web of creation, many physicists and astronomers have wondered at the extreme improbability of finding a universe as it is with a unique creature, man, at its hub capable of thinking about the meaning and origin of creation. This improbability is compounded by the multitude of rectifying steps beginning with the chaos of the early Universe and extending to the present state; these steps include the formation of the first stars, then the planets and among them the Earth, the emergence of life, then the ebb and flow of the species and ultimately man. Each step is characterised by a move towards order rather than disorder as would be implied in the physical laws of thermodynamics. Yet despite this improbability, a creature capable of complex emotions, of philosophy and of prayer has emerged on the scene. Scientists have puzzled over the unlikeliness of each step; yet how much more unlikely would be the whole sequence of steps each resolved in such a way as to lead to man. The improbability of it all is overwhelming.

In an attempt to reconcile these problems the Anthropic Principle was enunciated. As originally stated this was, 'The Universe must be such as to admit conscious beings in it at some stage'. In other words, a world capable of producing systems of the complexity and adaptability of conscious beings must be very tightly knit in its structure — it has a very particular character in its laws and a delicate balance in its fundamental forces.

In the last 20 years the special global conditions in the Universe necessary for the formation of life have been recognised. The most important is the fine balance between the explosive expansion of the Universe and its gravitational attraction; too much gravity would result in the contraction of the Universe in too short a time for life to form, too great an explosion would lead to a world too tenuous for any of the critical processes to occur. Many other conditions are required of the fundamentals of the Universe; for example if the relative strength of the strong nuclear force which holds the nuclei of atoms together and the electromagnetic force between charged particles were different then carbon, an essential atom in life-forms, would not exist.

An alternative approach, and one which attempts to avoid the implications of the Anthropic Principle, is to suggest that there might be a portfolio of many different universes of which ours happens to be the one containing conscious beings. Perhaps there is an infinite series of universes, each arising from the oscillations of one universe which has been for ever expanding and contracting through an infite past. Then on one of these oscillations a universe, the one we know, emerges containing *Homo sapiens*. This speculation about an infinity of universes is no more attractive and may be less attractive to many scientists and philosophers than the picture of delicate balance implicit in the Anthropic Principle.

At one stage in the development of the dialogue between science and religion there was a tendency to ascribe to God only those aspects of creation on which scientists could shed no light. This approach was rightly ridiculed later as pointing to a 'God of the gaps' whose sovereignty would diminish with the advance of scientific knowledge. One of the merits of the Anthropic Principle is that it helps us see how God can be at work in areas accessible to science rather than only in the gaps in our knowledge.

Why then are the laws of science as they are? Will scientists be able to discover the unifying principle which holds together all aspects of this grand design? The answers to such questions lie in the future. What can be said now is that the answers will in no way diminish the Creator.

Questions for Discussion

1. The argument in the section 'Creation out of nothing' will be new for many Christians. Does it disturb our traditional understanding of God?

2. '... the fullest way of understanding God in his creation is to know Jesus...' Why and how does our knowledge of Jesus help us to see the hand of God in the creative process?

3. Is it helpful to think of God creating a world full of potential for growth and development rather than a world in which every detail is fore-ordained?

4. Does not the short time human beings have been on Earth in comparison with the age of the universe, and the size of the uninhabited universe, suggest a rather wasteful Creator?

CHAPTER FIVE

EVOLUTION

THOMAS HUXLEY, the great evolutionary biologist, was once asked what he thought it was possible to conclude about God from a study of the natural world, and is said to have replied, 'an inordinate fondness for beetles'. It was an understandable remark as there are some half a million different kinds of beetle, over a third of all known species of animal life. This is an astonishing level of diversity and, at first sight, the only possible reaction for a biologist seeking to understand it all would seem to be utter despair.

However, if we take a closer look, we find that there is a great deal of order and structure amid all this diversity. The very fact that we can talk meaningfully about beetles shows that all beetles share some common characteristics that enable us to place them in a single group of that name. Other animal species also fall into groups and we find that these groups can be placed together in further, larger groups. Thus the groups 'beetles', 'flies', 'wasps' and 'butterflies' can all be put together in a larger group called insects, while 'mammals', 'birds', 'reptiles' and 'fish' can be grouped together in the larger group called vertebrates (animals with backbones). These groupings can be shown in a diagrammatic form:

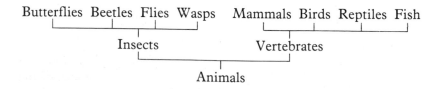

The diagram makes no attempt to show all the different types of grouping of the animal kingdom, but illustrates some relationships in what is a very complex pattern.

This kind of classification of animals looks rather like a family tree and so it is natural to ask whether or not it really does represent a family tree. Was there, in the distant past, a 'great, great grandfather' animal from which modern animals are all descended?

Various people over the years tried to answer this question, but it was Charles Darwin who, in the middle of the last century, gave a resounding 'yes', and backed up his answer with some compelling evidence.

Firstly, Darwin argued that this kind of development, which is known as evolution, had in fact occurred during the history of the earth. To do this, he drew on four main lines of evidence:

1. **Fossils.** The record of ancient animal forms that are preserved as fossils shows that different animals lived at different times in the past. Furthermore, it can be seen that groups appeared in the order you would expect if life had evolved: in very old rocks, the only fossil vertebrates are primitive fish; later the amphibia appear, followed by reptiles and finally mammals.

2. **Anatomy.** The reason it is possible to classify animals as above is that the animals in each group share a similar structure that is unique to the group. Thus, all land vertebrates share a common limb structure with one bone in the upper part of each limb and two in the lower part. It is difficult to understand why this should be so, unless they had evolved from a common ancestor.

3. **Embryology.** The early embryos of animals are often very similar, even when the adult forms are very different. The early embryos of human beings, for example, are very similar to those of other mammals and reptiles and it is only in later development that they become different. Again, this would be rather surprising if some form of evolution had not taken place.

In some cases, the difference between the adult structures that develop from very similar embryonic structures is enormous. For example, the tiny bones of the middle ear of mammals develop from the same embryonic bones that, in a reptile, form the joint where the lower jaw meets the skull. Why should this happen unless at some time in the past these bones changed their function?

4. **Rudimentary Organs.** Why do some snakes have leg bones contained entirely within the main part of their bodies? The simplest explanation is that their ancestors had legs like lizards but these were gradually lost as they took up a new lifestyle.

Secondly, Darwin clinched his argument by providing a mechanism for this evolutionary change. The offspring of animals (or any other type of living organism) are varied and so some of them will be better adapted to their environment than others. For example, a lion that can run a little faster than other lions will be better at catching gazelles. These will be the individuals which survive and reproduce and so pass on their improved characteristics to the next generation. Thus, over time, animals will gradually become better and better adapted to their environment, or, if the environment changes, they will be able to respond to those changes. As an analogy, Darwin pointed to animal breeders who select the best varieties of cattle or dogs and use them to sire the next generation. Over time (a minute length of time compared with the age of the Earth), as a result of this artificial selection, breeders have created the vast range of dog breeds, from Pekinese to Afghan hounds. In the wild it is nature which selects the best individuals, a process which Darwin called natural selection.

When Darwin was writing he faced two major difficulties with his ideas on evolution. First, he had very little knowledge of the process of heredity; how does variation arise and how is it passed on to offspring? In the succeeding 120 years, the science of heredity, genetics, has developed and completely vindicated Darwin. It is now largely understood how natural selection works at the molecular level.

Furthermore, advances in molecular genetics have made it possible to compare the genetic material, generally DNA (see p. 53), in different organisms. If this is done, it is found that there is a close relationship between the extent of the differences in this material and the length of time since the ancestral lines of the organisms are likely to have separated (inferred from the fossil record and the classification described earlier). Thus, modern genetics has provided a powerful new means of classification. This has not only assisted scientists in their attempts to classify organisms, but has also provided a direct physical link between the genetic changes of evolution and the patterns of classification which led us to think in evolutionary terms in the first place.

Darwin's other difficulty was that the fossil record was not as good as he would have liked. It did not seem to show a continuous development of animals from a single common ancestor to the range of modern forms; instead there were embarrassing gaps. However, this is not nearly so large a problem as it might seem at first sight. The fossil record is inevitably very patchy; it is estimated that there have been some four billion species of animals and plants alive at some time during the history of the earth, while only about 250,000 (0.006%) are known as fossils. Hence, many gaps are inevitable. Also, some of the crucial gaps have been filled by recent finds. For example, it was mentioned above that the bones of the reptilian jaw had developed into those of the middle ear of mammals. This might seem to be an extraordinarily unlikely change, but a good sequence of fossils has shown how it happened. A group of animals, called the mammal-like reptiles, gradually became more mammal-like around 250-200 million years ago. During this time one of the bones of the lower jaw, the dentary, grew bigger and bigger while the other bones became smaller and smaller. Eventually, the dentary became so big that it came up against the skull and formed a second jaw joint alongside the original joint, rather like two hinges on a door. Thus, 200 million years ago, there lived a group of small, shrew-like creatures, with a double jaw joint. The early mammals probably detected vibrations when they rested their heads on the ground, so vibrations were already being transmitted through the jaw joint. Once a second joint had formed, the first was free to specialise in hearing, both from the ground and from the eardrum which was close to the jaw joint. Darwin knew little of this spectacular sequence of fossils.

Since he wrote his seminal book, *On the Origin of Species*, the evidence in favour of Darwin's ideas has become overwhelming and, while some of the details of the mechanism are hotly debated, virtually no one who has studied the subject doubts the central ideas. It is a powerful and inspiring theory which not only explains the structure of modern and fossil organisms but also enables us to make sense of the extraordinary diversity of life.

Despite this there are some today who call themselves creationists, believing that the origin of the world and living things was more or less as told in the stories in the book of Genesis. They claim that the world is only five or ten thousand years old and was brought suddenly into being in its present form. Their influence is seen in the insistence that 'creation science' should be taught in the schools of some American states. Clearly, this view is incompatible with the evolutionary view defended above in which living forms developed over many hundreds of millions of years. Ironically modern creationism is descended from views that were discredited well before Charles Darwin began to formulate his ideas on evolution. In the early nineteenth century geologists realised that the world must be very old indeed and maintained this view alongside their traditional Christianity.

Though the argument between creationists and others is usually couched in scientific language and is presented as being about the nature of the universe it is frequently in fact about the nature of God. No evidence is really relevant to the discussion, for it would be possible for a creationist to agree fully with the facts offered as evidence of evolution by Darwin or anyone else but to claim that the world was created by God in 4004 BC with its fossil record and other features explained by Darwin's theory already in place. What God's reasons might be for such an action are a matter for speculation.

Ultimately therefore creationism must be answered on theological not scientific grounds. The God of creationism is a deceiver and a cheat. He gives us powers of sight, touch, hearing, taste and smell, but creates a world in which we cannot believe the evidence of our senses. He gives us minds but forbids us to use them to their full potential.

On the other hand the God of science invites us to explore and enjoy his creation without reserve. He is a creative God as the processes of evolution are creative. As we have seen elsewhere in this book, the physical world contains a mixture of chance and necessity; the chance interactions of particles and molecules are governed by the necessity of simple physical laws. In the living world, random variation (chance) combined with natural selection (necessity) has produced the evolutionary process, which culminated in the emergence of people. Thus there is inbuilt into the structure of the universe a remarkable creativity which contained the potential for the emergence of mankind. Just as an acorn contains the potential to develop into a magnificent oak tree, so the Big Bang contained the seeds of conscious life. It would not have been possible to predict where and when life would emerge, but that it would do so could be claimed with confidence. As Darwin himself commented, 'There is grandeur in this view of life'.

The word 'emergence' was used for people deliberately because we represent a new departure for the universe. We have emerged *from* the natural world in the sense that we have escaped from some of its constraints. Modern medicine and technology mean that natural selection no longer has the hold over us that it once did; many individuals who would once have died may now survive and reproduce. And we have emerged *into* a new realm as we have acquired new properties — a high level of consciousness, religious awareness and moral responsibility — which set us apart from the rest of creation. It is these properties, which emerged from the wholly natural process of evolution, which give us the possibility of living a life that reflects the nature of the One who was, when creation began.

Questions for Discussion

1. Darwin said of the creativity built into the structure of the universe, 'There is a grandeur in this view of life.' What do you think he meant by that? Do you agree?

2.   How does the idea of evolution seem to threaten traditional Christian faith?

3.   How can you reconcile the picture of a creation in which the rule is the survival of the fittest, with the picture of a God who has a 'bias to the poor'? (See for example Isaiah 11.4, Luke 1.52-53, and Paul's first letter to the Corinthians 1.27-28).

4.   Is evolution as we understand it today based solely on chance? Can the random element in the universe be reconciled with the idea of a God who has a purpose in creation?

CHAPTER SIX

A CLOSER LOOK AT LIFE

IN EARLIER CHAPTERS we have used the word 'life' without pressing closely the question as to how it is to be defined. The question is not an easy one, and is rendered more difficult by the fact that we use the word in many different ways. Always the intention is to draw a sharp distinction between two conditions, living and dead, and this has led to a widespread belief that life is an additional attribute. Death on this view is the result of the loss of the vital element. This sort of explanation invites challenge by scientists who must ask 'Are we sure that we need a separable, extra entity of this kind? Could not life be simply a property of some form of substance or structure?' We shall look very briefly at the progress made in trying to answer these questions.

A dictionary offers a wide range of alternative meanings for the word 'life' and no progress is possible until we have defined the way in which we are going to use it. Our definition should ideally be applicable to the whole spectrum, from the simplest moulds and bacteria to human beings. We therefore define as 'living' any structure which displays certain basic characteristics; it may be part of a larger structure, but must itself be a physically definable unit. It must interact with its environment, receiving 'food' in some shape or form; it may also receive energy, e.g. from light. It must be capable of growth, and the reproduction of its own structure. In this definition a complex structure such as an animal has life at several levels, culminating in that of the creature as a whole.

This approach to the subject prompts the question as to how far we need to probe into the make-up of an animal before we come to units which no longer display life as we have defined it. (The situation is roughly analogous to that of a mechanic dismantling a complex machine; sub-units such as a gear box are recognisable entities, but pursued too enthusiastically the break-up yields ultimately a heap of parts, the purpose of which is not immediately apparent.) An important stage in the analysis of any animal or plant is the cell. This is already known to be very small; typically a billion (1,000,000,000) weigh less than a pound and each is much too small to be seen with the naked eye. Yet they are certainly alive in the sense of our definition. Indeed very many of them exist as independent single cells, in the form of moulds, bacteria, amoebae, etc. These formed the earliest recognisable form of life and have remained quantitatively the most successful. Bacteria have proved capable of adapting to extremely hostile environments and unpromising diets. It is estimated that despite their minute size, single-celled organisms still constitute something like 90% (by weight) of all living matter on the earth today.

What do we know about these micro-organisms which consist of single cells? Although tiny by human standards, the cell contains a complex world within its outer skin (membrane). We can identify microscopically a range of smaller structures, many enclosed by their own membranes and all immersed in a fluid in which a variety of chemical substances are dissolved. All these membranes act as selective barriers, permitting some chemical substances to flow through them, but restricting others. In particular the outermost membrane not only maintains the identity of the cell, but acts as the gateway through which the cell exchanges material with its environment. Within the cell, complex chemical processes continually occur, in which the several types of sub-unit each have their own particular functions. The cell can properly be thought of as analogous to a large industrial complex, comprising a series of separate units which operate in a coordinated way to produce a range of intermediates and ultimately one or more final products. However the chemistry of the cell is altogether more complex and elegant than any yet contemplated in a human design. We have to ask what causes these complex chemical reactions to occur and how they are controlled.

The cell depends for its existence on food which it receives from its environment, through its outer skin. This has to provide both the energy and the raw materials needed for the chemical reactions we observe. Many of these individual reactions have been identified and some of them carried out in the laboratory. There is no evidence that they differ essentially from reactions not related to living matter. The uniqueness of the overall cell chemistry lies in the way in which this complex system is controlled. As a rough analogy we can say that the cell contains the equivalent of the programme in a computer. At the descriptive level we identify this control mechanism in terms of chromosomes.

At the biochemical level we can give a more detailed account, involving the substances DNA and RNA. RNA is an abbreviation for ribonucleic acid, DNA for deoxyribonucleic acid. Except in the simplest cells (which do not have a separate nucleus), DNA molecules are found exclusively in the nucleus of the cell, where they form the structures we call chromosomes. A DNA molecule is rather like a long ladder in form, but one which is twisted into a spiral — the 'double helix'. Different sections of the molecule, known as genes, control the formation of different types of protein molecules, each of which plays a different part in the life of the cell — e.g. forming part of the cell structure or bringing about a particular chemical reaction. When a protein molecule of a particular type is to be synthesised, an RNA molecule with a structure determined by the relevant gene is first synthesised alongside this gene and then moves out of the nucleus into the outer part of the cell. There it causes many small amino-acid molecules which are already present in the cell to link up in a particular order and so form one molecule of the required protein.

The analogy between the cell and an industrial complex fails in one important way. The industrial complex is a permanent structure in which a desired process is carried out. In total contrast, a major part of the activity of the cell is concerned with reproducing itself from within. Here too the DNA molecules play a central part. Each double helix first splits down the middle to produce two 'half ladders', each consisting of one side of the ladder with half of each rung attached to it. Small molecules from within the cell then become attached to the half rungs until each 'half ladder' is built up into a complete replica of the original double helix. In this way the cell acquires two sets of DNA molecules. It then divides into two, each a complete cell with one complete set of DNA.

This account of life is intellectually satisfying, and it is especially noteworthy that no need has been found to invoke any new forces or influences to supplement our biochemistry, but it does leave us with a profound problem. Given one cell in an appropriate environment we can describe in ever-growing detail how additional cells will arise. But how did the first cells originate? There are three kinds of answer:

1. Random reactions of simple molecules happened by chance to produce enough of the essential compounds, including the present form of control mechanism, to make possible a first (perhaps crude) cell.

2. Gradual evolution occurred through less refined control mechanisms, long since superseded by the much more efficient one we now observe.

3. The first cells were the immediate outcome of a specific act of divine creation.

Of these, the third is clearly inconsistent with the point of view developed in this book. Scientists are committed to the objective of exploring how our present world may have arisen from the Big Bang without specific interventions to overcome awkward problems. Our assessment of the first answer requires us to judge the probability of so much complex chemistry having occurred by purely random meetings of molecules. On any plausible basis of calculation we have to conclude that this hypothesis cannot be right. So we are left to look for control mechanisms of the kind suggested in answer 2 above. This search goes on, with the hope and indeed confidence that a satisfying answer will be found. (A very readable account of the problem and one possible answer — using clay minerals as the original controller — is given by A. G. Cairns-Smith in his book *Seven Clues to the Origin of Life*).

Development of plants and animals

At first sight bacteria, plants and animals appear to have little in common beyond the fact that all are alive in their own ways. Closer inspection reveals a strong family connection; plants and animals consist of cells, similar in many ways to one another and to the single cell of a bacterium. But, unlike bacteria, all but the smallest plants and animals are made up of many cells. Roughly speaking, these cells play the part of bricks in the building of a wide variety of structures. Every cell uses essentially the same kind of chemistry controlled by the same sort of mechanism. The number of cells in a creature the size of an adult human is astronomical — of the order of 100,000,000,000 — each one with its internal control mechanism, and each subject to a constant process of decay and renewal.

In most many-celled species, each single plant or animal starts off as a single cell formed by the union of two germ cells, one from a male and one from a female. Each of these germ cells contains a half-set of DNA molecules, so that the fertilised cell they produce has a complete set (the 'recipe' for the new individual), derived equally from the father and from the mother. (Asexual growth of a single unfertilised cell — parthenogenesis — is found in some species). In either case the one cell divides repeatedly, and the resulting group of cells becomes an embryo, whose subsequent development leads to an independently living creature closely resembling the parents. To achieve this, cells must develop in a manner dictated by their location in the embryo. There is evidence here of a wider ranging form of control, instructing the cell's internal control how to proceed for the benefit of the larger structure. So some cells are at this stage instructed to start forming arms, other (similar) cells to form legs, a head, and so on. The individual cell is versatile; its programme is adjusted to satisfy the wider need of the developing creature. This adjustment is not a once for all operation; throughout the process of development some cells die and are replaced from within. The overall life of the complete individual represents an amazing piece of organisation. Research into the mechanisms involved is proceeding apace.

Does this description contradict a religious view of life? Generations of preachers have declared that only God can create a living being. However our understanding of the chemistry of life is such that it can be only a matter of time before it is possible to reproduce, in the laboratory, processes which amount to the creation of life as we have defined it. Indeed experiments have already taken place which are seen to show how the basic elements of life can be brought into being by human activity.

However there does not need to be a conflict here. By showing how living things are composed of elements already present in the universe, scientific enquiry suggests that the creator of the physical universe and of the living things within it is one and the same. It is not the creation of life which is a uniquely remarkable activity, but creation itself. Scientific enquiry reveals the nature of the creative process. Many will find it appropriate that a universe for which God is responsible is itself the source of so much creativity. Christians should see this creative activity as a sign of a living God.

Questions for Discussion

1. Has this chapter undermined the view that only God can create life?

2. The chapter says that living creatures are frequently composed of smaller living units, yet the whole is greater than the sum of the parts. Some animal communities, for example the population of a beehive or an ants' nest, can also be regarded as more than the sum of their members. What are the implications of this for our understanding of human society?

3. If life should be discovered elsewhere in the universe, how would this affect your view of God?

4. Can the argument of this chapter be reconciled with the picture of God given in the Bible, for example in Ezekiel 37.1-14, or John 11.38-44?

CHAPTER SEVEN

BODY, MIND AND SOUL

EACH ONE OF us has the sense of being a soul, a self, a person, a 'real me' who is somehow distinct from the body and able to direct it. It has also been usual, at any rate among Christians, to distinguish between the soul and the mind. This is not such an easy distinction, as we realize when we turn to the *Concise Oxford Dictionary*, which gives 'Soul, opp. to body' and 'Person, as embodying mental qualities' among the definitions of Mind, and 'Person viewed as embodying moral or intellectual qualities' among the definitions of Soul! However, the verbs we use when speaking of ourselves and our minds — I *am* a person, I *am* me, but I *have* a mind — suggest that we see the 'real me' as more than the mind. To say that someone 'has a good mind' tells us only about his or her intelligence — not about ability to relate well to other people, to love, to appreciate beauty, to respond to goodness, or to worship, which are attributes of the 'good person' or 'good soul'. And for the Christian, everyone is to be valued as a soul or person, however much the ability of his or her mind is limited by illness or handicap.

There is a widespread impression that this Christian belief in our significance as persons has been undermined by science, particularly by psychologists and psychiatrists who study the mind on the one hand, and neurophysiologists who study the nervous system on the other.

The approach of some psychiatrists and psychologists has been to interpret many or all the elements of religious faith as products of wishful thinking. We cherish the idea of God as father, they tell us, because as we grow up we discover the imperfections of our human parents; we hope for heaven as a way of coping with the seeming finality of death. These and similar claims appear to call into question the account which religion has traditionally given of the life of the human soul.

The neurophysiologists have shown that our sensations, thoughts, emotions and actions are all closely tied up with what happens in the brain. This organ consists mainly of a network of some several billion nerve cells (neurones) between which messages are transmitted. To enable this to happen, a typical neurone has a fibre (axon) arising from it and ending in branches whose tips make contact with other neurones. Messages travel as electric impulses along the axon to the tips of its branches, where they cause the release of minute quantities of chemicals which initiate or suppress similar impulses in the adjacent neurones.

Two main strands of evidence indicate that groups of neurones in different parts of the brain are linked to different aspects of mental function — some neurones at the back of the brain to vision, at its left side to recognition of word sounds, at its right side to musical appreciation, at its front to memory, at its top to movement, and near its centre to the emotions. One of the two strands of evidence is that these aspects of function suffer when the corresponding area of the brain is damaged — e.g. by a stroke or surgical operation. The other is that when an artificial stimulus — e.g. a minute electric impulse from a microelectrode — is applied to one of these areas, the patient may think he or she is experiencing sights, sounds, etc. depending on which area is stimulated.

Such findings suggest that every mental or spiritual experience involves physicochemical changes in a particular part of the brain, and raise the same question about the soul as was posed about life at the beginning of the last chapter; do we need a separable, extra entity of this kind? Could not the sense of being a person distinct from the body and able to control it be an illusion produced by the physicochemical changes in the brain that we have described?

In the nature of things this cannot be proved either way, just as we cannot prove or disprove that we alone exist and that when our senses tell us there is a universe all around they deceive us. However there are many distinguished psychiatrists and neurophysiologists who believe that we can usefully talk about the soul and that the sense we have of our own selves is not an illusion. Sir John Eccles for example, in *The Self and its Brain* by Sir Karl Popper and himself, argued that the 'self-conscious mind', 'self' or 'soul' is an autonomous reality which interacts with the body through neurones in the brain. More recently he has suggested how this might happen without violating the conservation laws of physics.

Whether or not Eccles' particular hypothesis is right, it would be a mistake to think of our minds or souls as nothing but electric impulses and molecules passing through and between neurones. The late Donald Mackay, Professor of Communication at the University of Keele and an authority on the functioning of the brain, used the phrase, 'nothing buttery' to describe the habit of assuming that when you have explained something you have explained it away. An electronics engineer can explain what is happening in a radio during a performance of Handel's *Messiah* in terms of electrons and magnetic impulses, but no one would say that the Oratorio was nothing but a pattern of electrons and magnetic impulses — or indeed that it was nothing but a lot of notes in a score of music.

It would be equally unhelpful to think of the electrons and magnetic impulses, the notes in the score and the impact which the music makes on the listener as three separate entities which together make up Handel's *Messiah*. Rather, they are three different ways of looking at the one work. In much the same way, we should think of body, mind and soul as three significant ways of looking at the one individual, rather than as three separate entities. As people we can be thought of in many ways and studied from many aspects, but these are all aspects of the one reality.

The intimate links that exist between the three aspects of body, mind and soul are perhaps most clearly seen in the context of disease, health and healing. A disorder in any aspect can reveal itself in any other. Disharmonious relationships can cause mental stress and physical illness. A person born with a mental or physical handicap can find it difficult to relate satisfactorily to other persons. An accident can result in a coma during which the connection between body and soul appears to be broken. Drugs can induce or help to heal disharmony, as for example in the case of schizophrenia. Brain surgery can alter personality. Mental illness can reduce a person's ability to make moral choices. Suffering can enrich or disfigure a soul.

As sickness reaches every aspect of the patient, so too should the healer. The aim of healing is to make whole, not only dealing with sickness in one aspect but bringing every aspect together in harmony. The healer who thinks of patients as only bodies runs the risk of thinking of them as mere machines, which have broken down because of a fault in one component or another which the healer's job is to find (diagnose) and mend (treat). This view is reinforced by the modern image of high-technology medicine in which patients are attached by tubes and wires to banks of computers and other gadgetry which look more like the cockpit of Concorde than a place where sick people are made whole. Of course such medical technology is vital, but it must not blind the healer to the patient's need for health of mind and soul as well as of body.

This need is in some ways harder to meet because some healers (e.g. physicians and surgeons) must be concerned mainly with the impact of disease on the body, others (e.g. psychologists and psychiatrists) with its impact on the mind and others (e.g. ministers of religion and counsellors) with its impact on the soul. However, there are those who are moving towards a more holistic approach which recognizes the interdependence of body, mind and soul and the importance of collaboration between healers of different kinds. We are even beginning to acknowledge the interdependence of patient and healer.

This has particular implications for healers who see their task primarily as ministering to the soul. Leslie Weatherhead wrote, 'The forgiveness of sins is the greatest therapeutic idea in the world.' Religious language may give the impression that souls are to be saved out of the world of space and time, but if the aim of religion is the health of the soul this ought not to be considered apart from the health of the entire person. (For a fuller discussion of the concept of soul and its relevance to healing see the essay by William Strawson in *Mental Health and the Church*, published by the Methodist Division of Social Responsibility.)

The word soul is frequently used in the context of a discussion about life after death. As we have emphasised the interdependence of body, mind and soul, is it possible to envisage a soul when physical and mental processes have come to an end? Let us try a purely fanciful illustration. Imagine Pythagoras seated on some ancient shore, writing in the sand with a stick. Suddenly at the end of a prolonged calculation a flash of inspiration strikes him and he draws in the sand a right-angled triangle. Under it he adds the legend, 'The square on the hypotenuse equals the sum of the squares on the other two sides.' At that moment a great wave washes in and obliterates every mark on the sand. What has happened to Pythagoras' theorem? Nothing. The wave has merely washed his notes away. The facts he discovered about right-angled triangles existed long before Pythagoras proved them. Though we cannot locate them in time and space, we cannot deny their truth. At any time they may be expressed again in an appropriate medium, whether clay or pen and ink. So we may expect that the real person who takes one form in the universe we know, may be recreated in an appropriate manner in that other realm about which we know little except that it is where God's love rules and which we are glad to call heaven.

Earlier in this chapter we described body, mind and soul as three significant ways of looking at the one person. In Christian terms they are all important but not equally important, the soul is dominant. The most significant thing about us is that we are open to God. There are many ways of valuing people, according to their abilities, their wealth, their achievements and so on, but the declaration that someone is a soul gives that person a value which is unique and which cannot be surpassed.

Questions for Discussion

1. What do you mean when you use the words 'mind' and 'soul'?

Do these both refer to the same part of our being, and if not how do they differ?

2. Can people who are mentally ill be held responsible for their actions? How should we deal with criminals who are suffering from a mental disorder? Is a mental illness such as depression a sign of lack of faith?

3. How can the church give more attention to the ministry of healing?

4. How can we express the idea of God's love to people who are severely handicapped?

CHAPTER EIGHT

FREE WILL AND PROVIDENCE

THE DEGREE TO which we are free to make meaningful choices in life is a puzzle which has exercised the minds of thinking people down the centuries. A further question for a religious person, sharpened by recent studies in psychology and the functioning of the brain, is how God can bring his influence to bear on people and events.

In the ancient world the questions hardly ever arose. On the one hand, it was understood that gods, including the God of the Old Testament, were all-powerful and could intervene in the created world whenever they so wished. They could suspend the laws of nature, bring about apparently miraculous events, and express their pleasure or displeasure through the elements present in the created world. On the other hand, it was generally assumed that human beings had freedom of choice. Free will is implicit in the whole of the Bible record, so that people are always held to be fully responsible for their actions and the consequences. Indeed without the idea of free will such concepts as remorse, repentance, reward and punishment, cease to have much meaning. These ideas went unchallenged for many centuries. To some degree they still persist. Many people still think of God as an external agent who can be persuaded to intervene in natural events. The concept of personal responsibility for action, with some qualification, remains the basis of the criminal law, which judges all persons to be fully accountable for their actions.

By the seventeenth century, these ideas came under increasing suspicion, as a consequence of dramatic developments in understanding the nature of the physical world. The application of Isaac Newton's ideas revealed a mechanical universe with a high degree of order and predictability. The nature of matter and energy were better understood; the motions of heavenly bodies could be predicted with elegance and accuracy. From this new concept of order and predictability, the idea of determinism began to develop, though Newton himself never abandoned his belief in God. It was towards the end of the eighteenth century that Laplace gave forceful expression to the concept of a closed universe. He visualised every atom as moving along a path uniquely determined by the forces acting upon it; if the position, motion, and system of forces were known, the whole future of the atom was determined. There was a rigid framework of cause and effect. If for one atom, then similarly for all atoms, and so the idea of kinetic-corpuscular determinism was born. There was thus no need for God, except perhaps as a kind of retired engineer.

The idea of determinism in the physical world soon spread into the realm of ethics. In this context the proposition in its most extreme form is that all moral decisions are the result of previously existing mental, physical, or environmental causes. On this basis human beings had little choice or responsibility and God seemed irrelevant, and the stage was set for serious conflict between science and religion.

All this was drastically changed by the revolution of scientific thought and understanding that has occupied most of the twentieth century, and is still proceeding. The elucidation of the structure of matter on the microscopic scale, developments in cosmology, and far-reaching enlargement of our knowledge concerning the nature of life, have presented a new climate of thought. Some of these have immediate relevance to the present discussion.

The quantum theory has exposed an inherent uncertainty in physical processes at subatomic levels. For example as Werner Heisenberg has shown, it is not possible to measure both the position and the velocity of a particle at one instant of time, not because the measurement is inaccurate but because measuring the one changes the other. Observer and observed cannot be separated. Further, the behaviour of any individual particle is unpredictable, and the laws of nature on a microscopic scale are only observable as the expression of the average behaviour of a large number of particles. In this sense, for the individual particle, determinism is dead. Moreover, considerations of relativity theory lead to the conclusion that the sequence of events in the space-time continuum can be modified by the position of the observer. The relationship between cause and effect as commonly understood in terrestrial events is not as simple as has hitherto been assumed.

We therefore need to consider whether this new-found latitude in the physical world has a parallel that applies to moral issues. Certainly it would be wrong to go to the extreme of libertarianism, which postulates that human beings are totally free to choose a course of action at any moment without being influenced by their past history or present circumstances. The physical equivalent of that would be chaos and no scientist could accept that. But is this freedom we seek to identify real or illusory, complete or qualified? We need to recognise a middle position between total freedom and determinism. There is a clue in some lines from Brian Wren's hymn.

> *Half-free, half-bound by inner chains,*
> *By social forces swept along*
> Hymns and Psalms 500

There are both inner and outward constraints. Heredity plays a part; studies on twins suggest that even criminality can depend to some degree on a person's genes. Imbalance in the chemical composition of the body, and drugs, can bring about behavioural changes. External and social circumstances can exert considerable pressures. Human behaviour is highly complex and subject to many influences. Nevertheless, it is our common experience that in our day to day activity we do have both the opportunity and the responsibility of freedom of choice; to reject this and accept that, to say yes to some things and no to others. There is nothing in current scientific thinking that would contradict that.

What part does God play in this? We can believe that he is able to influence events in a world that he has created, but the model of an interventionist God should be replaced by the concept of a God who is always present and at work everywhere, best able to achieve his purposes by working through people who cooperate with him. The result of his influence is to help people see the pattern of his will more clearly, and to give them the strength of purpose to choose and to pursue what is right.

Along these lines it is possible to develop a concept of the tripartite relationship between God, human beings and the natural world, that is not inconsistent with modern scientific thinking, and that does not invalidate a belief in free will and providence.

It is sometimes said that God's omniscience takes away our freedom. If God already knows the future it must be illusory to imagine that we can change it. A simple illustration may help to show how this need not be so. A rower may be proceeding downstream, unaware that round the next bend in the river are dangerous rapids. Overhead a helicopter pilot is able to look down and see both the rower and the rapids. He has the advantage of an extra dimension. The pilot sees where the rower is heading, in a real sense he sees the rower's future. However the rower is still free to influence that future by whether he rounds the bend cautiously or recklessly, or whether he heeds or ignores any warnings the helicopter pilot may shout.

There remains the question of whether men and women are unique in being open to God's influence, or whether God can act directly on his creation without the need for human agency. On this topic many scientists remain agnostic. Investigation of the natural world and the physical universe has not revealed any power which needs to be labelled 'Spirit of God'. At the same time no scientist would claim to know all there is to know about the properties of the universe. Many have discovered that research into the nature of things can yield as many questions as answers and that they experience humility towards what they do not know as often as confidence about what they know.

However we do not want to repeat the mistakes of the past by trying to locate God in the areas of our ignorance. We are on safer ground in declaring that God's influence on the natural world is the order and design which has marked his creation from the beginning.

Whether or not it is legitimate to go beyond this, is something we shall consider as we turn to the subject of miracles.

Questions for Discussion

1. Are we more or less free than we commonly imagine? How can we increase the area of our freedom?

2. Does God guide us to the extent of overruling our free will? What does that say about God's attitude towards his creation?

3. Why should the model of an interventionist God be replaced by the concept of a God who is always present and at work everywhere?

4. How do you think of the relationship between God, human beings, and the natural world?

CHAPTER NINE

MIRACLE

Definition

We use the word miracle in many different ways. A policeman arriving at the scene of an accident may exclaim, 'It's a miracle no one was killed.' We speak of springtime as nature's annual miracle. The Bible records many miraculous events, and Christians have seen the miracles of Jesus as evidence of his divinity. Probably the word is most frequently used to describe something which cannot be explained or which appears contrary to the laws of nature as we understand them at present. In this sense the word is often used of healing when it takes place contrary to the expectations of doctors or surgeons.

The question posed by miracles for scientists and for Christians will depend on what we think a miracle is. For present purposes we define miracles in three ways.

a) They appear to contradict the laws of nature.

b) They evoke a sense of wonder and awe.

c) They point to the active involvement of God in his world.

All three parts of this definition have implications for our present study.

Contrary to the laws of nature

Scientists view the world as essentially reliable. It functions according to regular and predictable patterns. Without the assumption that the world is an orderly place, scientific enquiry would be impossible. The scientist believes that under the same circumstances matter will always behave in the same way. His observations about the way things behave are set down in the form of laws. What then can be made of an observation which appears to be incompatible with scientific explanation? The assumption must be either that the observations are inaccurate or that existing laws are not good enough, rather than that the laws have been broken. Much scientific progress has been the result of observations which do not fit in with existing laws. Laws are consequently modified or new laws are set down. For example, every student of physics has heard of Boyle's Law of the behaviour of gases. This states that for a fixed mass of gas at constant temperature the pressure multiplied by the volume is always the same. If you double the pressure you halve the volume. However as scientists were able to study the behaviour of gases over an increasing range of temperatures and pressures it was found necessary to modify Boyle's law to explain the properties of gases more accurately. This is a typical example of developments which, while useful, do not seriously affect our basic understanding.

Occasionally however a new observation seems to destroy the foundations on which we have hitherto relied. Such a situation arose in Manchester in 1910 when two of Ernest Rutherford's students fired a stream of α-particles at a thin gold sheet and observed, to their total astonishment, that while most of them went straight through, a few (about 1 in 8,000) actually bounced back. Rutherford's response was, 'It was almost as incredible as if you fired a 15″ shell at a piece of tissue paper and it came back and hit you.'

As a result of this, J. J. Thomson's 'plum pudding' model of the atom, where the negative ions were embedded in an evenly spread sphere of positively charged material, had to be changed drastically. It was replaced by the model of the nuclear atom in which all the positive charge and most of the mass is localised in a tiny nucleus only one forty thousandth of the diameter of the whole atom. The electrons are found in the rest of the atom which is mainly empty space.

Such a new observation properly called for a profound change of theory. The unacceptable alternative to making such a change would be to regard the observation as evidence of the occurrence of a miracle.

A sense of wonder

It is commonly assumed that when a scientific account has been given of an event which was previously thought to be miraculous, the element of wonder goes and the miracle ceases to be miraculous. This is not the experience of many scientists today who say that the more they know about the universe, the more they experience wonder and awe. Those with little or no scientific knowledge can feel wonder at the 'sonar' used by a bat to enable it to fly safely in the dark, at the size of the universe, and at the way in which all the characteristics of a particular human being can be contained within a single fertilised egg cell. So those who work on the frontiers of scientific knowledge report an increasing sense of wonder and humility. The discovery of an explanation for what is observed does not lessen their amazement at the nature of the universe, if anything it increases it.

In this they echo many of the earliest teachers and theologians who drew attention to the orderliness of the universe as a sign of God's creative care and a cause for wonder and thankfulness. It is a characteristic of human nature to be attracted by novelty, by the inexplicable and the unexpected. We ought however to be more impressed by the order and the design in the natural world. The amazing thing is that a fertilised egg can grow into a human being, and the more we know about that process, the more we are filled with a sense of awe.

Signs of God

New Testament writers see the things that Jesus did as signs of the nature and activity of God. Many of these were contrary to people's expectations and some of them were contrary to their current knowledge of the universe. They all caused surprise, whether Jesus was breaking social laws or natural laws. Sometimes that caused onlookers to see the hand of God in what Jesus was doing, with the result that they became his disciples.

Jesus himself took care to play down the wonderful nature of what he was doing. At the outset of his ministry he resisted the temptation to attract followers by a demonstration of supernatural power, and in the months that followed he refused invitations to perform miracles simply for effect. His actions caused surprise among people who had limited expectations of what was possible. He operated within the world view of his contemporaries, dealing with certain illnesses as signs of demon-possession for example, where we might want to give a different explanation. The aim of these actions was consistent, to reveal the nature of God, to offer fulness of life, and to establish God's rule over against the powers of disorder and death. He made it clear that this ministry was not his alone but was to be shared with his followers as a result of his death, resurrection and ascension.

As our knowledge of the universe has increased, so 'alternative' explanations of Jesus' miracles have been offered. These have been taken to exclude the necessity of seeing God at work in Jesus, and so scientific enquiry has been seen as a threat to religion. To this, religious people have responded in a number of ways, of which two deserve mention here.

The first is to assert that the laws of nature are God's laws and that he has therefore the right to suspend or override them to suit particular purposes. On this view scientific enquiry becomes irrelevant as we are dealing with causes which are not measurable in any way known to science. However such a view proves ultimately fatal to religion. As science eventually provides an explanation for what had previously been thought to be the inexplicable activity of God, so God becomes a hypothesis of which we have no need. There are also serious theological objections to this point of view. If God is capable of suspending his own laws he is seen to be capricious and inconsistent. Moreover one is bound to ask why he does not suspend his laws more often in order to prevent suffering and tragedy.

A second response has been to declare unreservedly that the laws of nature are part of God's creative design and that he is bound by them because they are part of himself. The discovery of a scientific law which accounts for something which was previously a mystery is not the discovery of an alternative explanation but the discovery of more about God. As we have already remarked the discovery of an aspect of the truth is as likely to evoke wonder and awe as is the sense of being baffled by the inexplicable. This wonder is an experience with which scientists are familiar.

There are many aspects of human experience which are not susceptible, or at least not wholly susceptible, to scientific enquiry. These include relationships, the appreciation of beauty, ethics, and the consideration of life's meaning and purpose. These are part also of God's creation and are ways in which he reveals himself and is involved in his universe. When discussing a miraculous event we shall need to remember that scientific enquiry will be relevant to part but not the whole of it.

Summary

The word miracle is used in many different ways. It should not be used to imply something which is opposed to a scientific view of the world, but rather to describe an event which by evoking wonder and awe takes us beyond a purely materialistic world view. Science itself no longer pictures the universe as a complex machine in which all events are entirely predictable. Rather scientific enquiry is a process in which greater knowledge leads to a new sense of mystery. The proper attitudes for the scientist is therefore one of openness and humility.

This sense of mystery should not lead us to speak of God only when we have no other explanations. Instead, God is to be adored as the creator of all things known and unknown, explicable and inexplicable. In areas where the sediment of ages has hidden from view the underlying bedrock, erosion may lead to the outcropping of that bedrock, thus revealing the fundamental structure of the local environment. So the events we call miraculous reveal what has always been true about God though these truths may have been hidden by the prosaic and the commonplace. It is in the discovery of the difference between our expectations and God's plan, between the forces of destruction and the Spirit of wholeness, that we experience that wonder and amazement that leads us properly to say 'It's a miracle!'

Questions for Discussion

1. The chapter offers a three-fold definition of miracle. Are you happy with that? If not, what is your definition?

2. In St. John's Gospel the writer says that miracles are signs which tell us something about God. What do we learn about God from (a) the miracle at Cana (John 2.1-11), (b) the healing of the disabled man (John 5.1-9), and (c) the resurrection of Jesus.

3. 'The laws of nature are God's laws' (page 71). Does this mean that he has the right to suspend them? How does your answer help you to understand the stilling of the storm recorded in Mark 4.35-41?

4. Can you give any examples of miracles that have happened in your own lifetime?

CHAPTER TEN

SUFFERING AND
NATURAL DISASTER

THE PROBLEM OF suffering is as old as the book of Job —
how can a caring God allow suffering in his creation? Or more
personally, why should a pious man like Job be put to so much
physical and mental anguish? Job's suffering was extreme, he was
so disfigured that his friends did not recognise him. In his agony
he cries out for release in death and in his extremity he rebels against
God. Seeking an explanation, the people around him ask if he has
secretly committed some wrong for which the suffering is a
punishment. Or is God chastising Job so that he might become a
more pious man? Is it the unholy Satan at work on the souls of man?
Or is this retribution for a weak faith easily broken by adversity?
Job's friends, representatives of the religious leaders and thinkers of
his day, offer false, contradictory, and generally unhelpful explanations
for the torment suffered by such a good man. Job cries out to God
that he created him only to tortue him. Despite the suffering of this
life Job sees one ray of hope that having enjoyed communion with
God on earth in the past, he might see a final justification after death.
But what of the providence of God? Job sees no clear answer.

We accept God as the creator of all the animate world of which man
is only a part. Do we face suffering as an inevitable part of God's
creation? This was a problem for Job and remains so for us today.
We will examine some aspects of this problem.

Man-made suffering
Firstly there is a major element of suffering in the human condition
that is self-inflicted or the consequence of individual or social neglect,
malice or just brute ignorance. Examples spring directly to mind.

We think of the abuse of our bodies and minds through what we eat, drink and smoke, knowing full well that smoking and some eating patterns go with an increased risk of heart disease, that smoking also leads to throat and lung cancer, and that social drugs can produce addiction with the attendant physical and mental degradation. Our actions have consequences, each course has its own result and there is no escape from it. We sow the wind and reap the whirlwind.

Is this the judgement of a God who delivers just deserts to a wilful and sinful world? This would have been the view of an Old Testament prophet like Ezekiel or Job's 'comforters' who saw that sin would bring its own suffering. In the New Testament however, God's love and redemptive power is emphasised, and we are invited to be agents of this redeeming activity by reducing or eliminating the causes of suffering which are within our own power. It is not only the function of the state to enact rules to govern our behaviour in a responsible way but it is also the individual's task to be his brother's keeper and to reduce these 'catastrophes' in individual lives, whether they be cancer, death or injury on the road, or the confused mind of the emotionally deprived child or adult. The fabric of the world is as it is and we have the power to order our lives accordingly.

Avoidable catastrophes

We can identify a second category of suffering — that which is noone's obvious fault, yet which could be prevented. This category includes the great famines of our time in Ethiopia, the Sudan and other areas of the southern Sahara which could be prevented by international collaboration. The sheer hopelessness of untold numbers of these famine victims has been brought strikingly into our homes by the medium of television. These images remind us that we are scarcely aware of what real suffering is like in our protected affluent Western world. Of similar magnitude is the distress produced by endemic diseases in many parts of the world. Malaria, typhoid and cholera are still rampant in many third world countries.

We look from a distance at this suffering and see the individual victim to be powerless in face of what he would see as misfortune or the hand of fate. From our perspective we also see remedies for these national disasters, disasters which are no longer a menace in countries with a high standard of living. Given adequate support, international organisations like the World Health Organisation and the UN Food and Agricultural Organisation could effectively eliminate the major endemic diseases and starvation. However the realisation of this aim depends on a commitment by the richer countries of the world to provide the considerable resources necessary, and in many cases political and social change within the receiving countries. It is our task as a Christian nation to face this responsibility squarely. We do not seem to be prepared to face the cost of a new international economic order which would help lift this burden from the shoulders of the developing world. The planet Earth can provide enough food for its present inhabitants; we have the resources in technology and know-how to eliminate starvation and eradicate many of the world's most common diseases. These catastrophes should no longer happen.

Suffering and catastrophes beyond our control
Thirdly, there is the suffering for which people can have no responsibility. At the individual level this includes some illness. For example some cases of disease start with damage to the DNA of a single cell by the background radiation, from space and within the earth's crust, to which we are all exposed. If a reproductive cell in the ovary or testicle is damaged in this way, the damaged DNA may be passed on to future generations and cause a hereditary disease such as haemophilia. If the cell affected is elsewhere in the body, it may multiply to cause a cancer.

Other causes of suffering which seem to lie beyond our control are storms, floods, earthquakes, tidal waves, lightning and the like, the events which insurance companies in their perversity call 'acts of God'. Within the fabric of the Earth we inhabit there is unstoppable catastrophe and crass brutish disaster, at least as seen from the human viewpoint. We are still awed by the immensity of the explosion of Mt. Vesuvius which destroyed Pompeii, not to mention the natural disasters of our own time — earthquake in Mexico, volcanic eruption in Colombia, escape of natural gases in Cameroun, floods in

Bangladesh, for example. Such catastrophes are part and parcel of creation.

There are other catastrophes of a much larger scale in the past history of our planet, events which we can be fairly certain will happen again. These include the recurrent ice ages whose origins are still not fully understood. During these ice incursions most plant and animal life is erased from intermediate and high latitudes. An ice age can be followed by flooding of great areas of the Earth as the ice melts.

Yet more drastic catastrophes occur on a global scale from time to time in the history of the Earth. These produce the mass extinctions of animal and plant life which punctuate the course of evolution on our planet. One of the most drastic occurred 65 million years ago in the period which marks the boundary between the geological Cretaceous and Tertiary eras. In this period the dinosaurs were entirely eliminated; the mammals emerged from this cataclysm and eventually came to dominate the Earth (in the form of human beings). Several mass extinctions have been identified in geological history; they last only a few million years and wipe out many of the species extant at that time. The events which can produce these large-scale changes on the surface of the Earth may originate in the Earth or may be extra-terrestrial. Major geological movements of the tectonic plates which underlie the continents can markedly change the shallow coastal waters or can throw large volumes of volcanic dust into the atmosphere which block out the heat-giving sunlight. Alternatively a large meteorite or comet striking the Earth would throw up a layer of dust so thick that it would block out sunlight and cause temporary freezing of the Earth.

On the longest time scales the Earth, Sun and the universe as we know it will come to an end. The Sun which provides the life-giving heat and light to the Earth will eventually use up all its hydrogen fuel and cool down, and life on it will come to an end. Astronomers are confident in predicting that this will not happen for about 5 billion years — for as long in the future as the Earth and Sun have already existed. Then the Earth will cool to near absolute zero ($-273°C$) where no life can exist. On an even longer time scale the universe will expand into emptiness with all the stars cooling to cinders. Then all will be darkness and cold. This is the end of the universe as astronomers see it.

Is there an answer?

What should our response as Christians be to this picture of an inevitable march of time in which species of animals and plants come and go, pushed hither and thither by forces of nature over which they seem to have no control? Firstly we should avoid glib, superficial or dishonest answers. Better to say nothing than to tell a lie. Secondly we must admit that much we have described counts as evidence against the picture of God that Jesus gives us. It may not be decisive evidence but evidence it is, and has to be taken seriously. Thirdly, it is relatively easy to see how some suffering arises as a consequence of human freedom. The first two categories of natural disaster discussed above occur as a result of the behaviour of people. As we have already seen, human life only really makes sense if we are, at least to some extent, free. But if we are genuinely free then there are bound to be occasions on which people abuse that freedom and do things that cause others to suffer. Clearly it is our responsibility to take what opportunities are open to us to care for those who suffer and to share in the struggle for justice.

At the other end of the spectrum of human involvement there are the natural disasters of the third category discussed above, such as earthquakes and floods, where it is not possible to blame the suffering on people at all. Here the problem is most acute for, if anyone is to blame, it must be God; but it is also here that the scientific view of the world might be most helpful in our efforts to understand suffering.

It is often assumed that God could create any kind of world. If he wished he could easily create a world that was just like our present one except that there were no earthquakes or floods. However, things may not be quite that simple. It has already been seen how the structure of the world can be characterised as a combination of chance and necessity, an interplay between the chance interactions of atoms and molecules and the necessity of physical laws. It is this interplay that makes the world such a creative place, that enables it to realise the enormous potential present within its origins in the Big Bang. Some authors have gone as far as to describe God's act of creation as a cosmic fugue, the working out of a vast range of variations on a simple theme.

Another important feature of the world is that it is very finely tuned. There are some physical constants which, if they were only very slightly different from their actual value, would result in the world being very different to the one we see. For example, the balance between the explosive force of the Big Bang and the strength of the force of gravity in the very early universe had to be almost equal for a world like our own to be created. If the force of gravity had been only very slightly weaker than it actually is, then matter would never have condensed into galaxies and stars, and so the Earth would never have taken shape. If gravity had been only very slightly stronger, the universe would soon have collapsed in on itself and there would have been no time for the Earth to form. The conclusion is that if the world is to be roughly like the one we have got then it has to be almost exactly like the one we have got. Varying any of the parameters, even by only an extremely small amount, results in a world that is very different and one that would not support life as we know it.

Taking these two features of the world together, it seems that we cannot pick and choose which features we would like. If the world is to be the kind of world that we have, one that is bubbling with creative possibilities, then it must also have features that we regard as unpleasant. Neither we nor God could have one without the other because they are logically connected. Not even God could create a world in which 1 + 1 = 3, and nor could God create a world with only the good aspects of our present world.

This view points towards an understanding of suffering in the world which sees it as an inevitable by-product of all that makes the world good. Evolution, the progress of creation, seems to be shot through with pain, sacrifice and blood. Like the travail of woman in birth, suffering seems to be inseparable from the creative life and growth around us. Paul recognises this groaning and travail of nature in his letter to the Romans. He accepts pain as a fundamental part of the process of birth and creation of a new order. So we must recognise that only in a world of chance and freedom can all the possibilities inherent in a structure of law and regularity be played out and developed; and that in a world of chance and freedom the operation of laws and regularity leads to accidents and suffering. Earthquakes are the price that we and God have to pay for all the possibilities of creativity and freedom.

Finally we must remember that one of the most revealing and enduring models of God is a man nailed to a cross. God shares in the life of his creation including its torment. But the cross is not the final picture the Bible leaves us with. Nearby is an empty tomb. God endures our pain and death but his final word is life. He invites us to look forward, not to the darkness and cold of a dying universe, but to the joy of heaven.

Questions for Discussion

1. Suffering, however caused, raises questions which need intellectual and pastoral answers. What is the difference?

2. Is it a satisfactory answer to the problem of suffering to speak about a redeemer God and our hope of heaven? If your answer is no, what is lacking?

3. Read Romans 8.18-25. How does Paul help us to come to terms with natural disasters? Who do you think Paul has in mind when he refers to the source of the suffering as 'him who made it so' (verse 20)?

4. In the Communion Service we pray that God will 'bring us with the whole creation' to his heavenly kingdom, implying that the whole creation is in need of salvation. Does this mean that earthquakes and floods are part of a fallen world, and why then should they have existed long before human beings walked the earth?

EPILOGUE

IN THE PRECEDING chapters we have tried to shed light on the methods of science and to give an account of current scientific thinking in a number of fields. The picture is not static, indeed some parts of our account may already be dated for we live in a period of intense scientific activity. It is the essence of the scientific approach to be willing to challenge even what seem to be the most fundamental and well established concepts in the face of new evidence.

This exciting world of new ideas and discoveries must be kept in perspective. For every person working at the frontiers of knowledge many more are employed in the application of useful discoveries. Nevertheless science looks forward in the search for a more profound understanding of our world as well as providing the tools for more confident and effective action in the present.

In contrast religion can appear to be backward looking. It speaks of a God who never changes. Its worship has deep roots in the past. Truths revealed thousands of years ago seem to carry more weight than those discovered yesterday or expected tomorrow. Yet religious people claim that the insights of their faith, no less than the fruits of scientific research, provide a valid basis for daily life. Is it possible to hold these two together and have a scientific as well as a religious attitude to life?

The thesis of this book is that it is not only possible but highly desireable and that the insights of science and faith can enrich each other. Just as our understanding of the world develops through the findings of scientific enquiry, so our understanding of God must be open to development in the light of experience. Our starting point is the Bible, complemented by the experience and judgement of believers through the centuries and by our own perceptions. In Jesus Christ we have the determinative picture of God, but that can be filled out as we discover his Spirit at work in the world and in ourselves.

In recent years the use that scientists have made of models has helped religious people to think more clearly about their faith. Much of the language of religion, if taken literally, seems absurd. How can God be one person and yet three persons? How can Jesus be both fully human and fully divine? How can millions of praying people be simultaneously in communication with God, and if they are why do they not all get the same answer? Our models of God may be crude but by using them we avoid the worse error of treating one picture as if it were the whole truth.

As our knowledge of science increases, so does our knowledge of God. Sometimes it is the discoveries of science that have compelled people to think again about God. For them the God of science and the God of faith begin to come together. That is as it should be if we believe that God is creator and that the universe reflects his nature. What is important is to find how to affirm the truths of science and religion in ways that honour them both.

The task is important and urgent, for the well-being of this and future generations depends on our being able to combine the fruits of science and technology with the vision of faith and the energy of prayer. If we are to end the situation in which food surpluses are destroyed in some countries while millions of people starve to death in others, we shall need both unlimited enthusiasm for the task and the best of use of people's economic and political acumen. If we are to avoid ecological disaster through the destruction of rain forests, the erosion of arable land, the exhaustion of fossil fuels or the pollution of our air and water, we shall need the will and the skill to live in a spirit of interdependence with all creation.

Both will and skill are from God. He meets us in prayer and he is discovered through research. He grants us the vision and he entrusts us with the power. He is Lord of all but he chooses to exercise this authority through people who trust him, people who are free not to trust him if they so choose.

How do we make sure that our freedom is available for God to use? In the course of his Vice-Presidential address to the Methodist Conference the late Dr. Russell Hindmarsh, then Professor of Atomic Physics at Newcastle University, posed this question and reminded

his hearers that when Jesus' disciples asked, 'What must we do if
we are to work as God would have us work?' the answer was simple
and direct. 'This is the work that God requires, believe in the one
[...]od has sent.'

[...] whole thrust of the New Testament is that people open
[...]ves in their freedom to God by committing themselves as
[...]s of Jesus who in a unique way is 'in the father'. Jesus is God
[...]te, confirming the worthwhileness of his creation and
[...]ing the integrity of nature. He will not turn stones into bread,
[...]oblem of hunger will not be solved by magic. He will not throw
[...]elf down from the Temple roof. God cannot suspend the
[...]amics of the physical world without utterly destroying the
[...]nomy which he himself gave to the universe. Jesus will not bring
[...]self down from the cross, for most of all he respects human
[...]dom, even the freedom to kill the Son of God.

[...]hroughout this book we have challenged the idea that science
[...]d religion occupy wholly different realms with no point of contact
[...]tween them. The nature of the relationship is not an easy one to
[...]efine precisely, though it arises out of the conviction that the God
of science and the God of faith are one and the same. So, we might
add, are the God of art, of music, of society, of politics and of poetry.
These activities are engaged in by people exercising their freedom
within the given structure of the world. God invites us to use our
freedom in certain ways and not in others; to apply the resources
of science to feeding hungry people rather than destroying life in
a nuclear catastrophe; through art to lift up the human spirit rather
than degrading it; by means of political judgement to enable all people
rather than a few to enjoy the benefits society offers to its members.

At the conclusion of his address Professor Hindmarsh invited those
present to address themselves to the great problems of the age. 'The
God we declare', he said 'is not content with the world as it is; he
hates the massive inequalities between the rich and the poor of the
world; he does not want to see the world made uninhabitable by
pollution or overpopulation. But the God we declare will not cure
these ills by magic; he believes in and respects the marvellous order
and symmetry of the natural world; he honours the freedom and
integrity of human beings even when they deny him; he expects his
people, the community of believers, to use their freedom in co-

operation with the structure of nature to reflect his character in society, and he declares himself to us in Jesus, setting his seal on his own creation and making it possible for us to do his will, through faith in Jesus as his Son. And that is why I profess physics and Christ.' His words have a timeless quality and make a conclusion to this book.

BIBLIOGRAPHY

THIS LIST includes the books specifically referred to in the text, together with a number which can be recommended for further study by those who wish to look further into matters of science and faith.

David Attenborough	*Life on Earth*	Fontana-Collins
D. J. Bartholomew	*God of Chance*	SCM
A. G. Cairns-Smith	*Seven Clues to the Origin of Life*	Cambridge
Fritjof Capra	*The Tao of Physics*	Fontana
Paul Davies	*God and the New Physics*	Dent
Richard Dawkins	*The Blind Watchmaker*	Longman
Laurie R. Godfrey	*Scientists Confront Creationism*	Norton
Stephen Jay Gould	*The Flamingo's Smile*	Penguin
Richard E. Leakey	*The Making of Mankind*	B.B.C. Publications
Donald McKay	*The Clockwork Image*	Inter-Varsity Press
Hugh Montefiore	*The Probability of God*	S.C.M.
Arthur Peacocke	*God and the New Biology*	Dent
John Polkinghorne	*One World*	SPCK
John Polkinghorne	*Science and Creation*	SPCK
Karl Popper and John Eccles	*The Self and its Brain*	Springer International
David M. Raup	*The Nemesis Affair*	Norton
Stuart Roebuck (ed)	*Christ and the Cosmos*	Westminster College
Michael Ruse	*Darwinism Defended*	Addison Wesley

Carl Sagan	*Cosmos*	B.B.C. Publications
Maurice Wiles	*God's Action in the World*	SCM
Christopher Wiltsher	*Everyday Science, Everyday God*	SCM

MEMBERS OF THE WORKING PARTY

David Bridge, B.A., B.D. (Chairman)
*Methodist minister and a Secretary of the Home Mission Division.
From September 1988 a circuit minister in Epsom.*

John F. Chapman, B.Sc., Ph.D.
*33 years work in Atomic Energy and Polyurethane Polymer
Industries.*

Geoffrey Clark
*Methodist minister and Superintendent of the Bramhall Circuit.
From September 1988 Chairman of the Nottingham and Derby
District of the Methodist Church.*

Rodney D. Davies, Ph.D., D.Sc., F.R.A.S.
*Professor of Radioastronomy, University of Manchester. President
of the Royal Astronomical Society. Methodist local preacher.*

Michael Davis, B.Sc., Dip.Ed., C.Chem., F.R.S.C.
*Head of Science, Cheadle Hulme School. Involved in Royal Society
of Chemistry, examining. Methodist local preacher.*

Allen Dinsdale, O.B.E., M.Sc., F.Inst.P., Hon. F.I. Ceram., F.R.S.A.
*Was Director of the British Ceramic Research Association.
Methodist local preacher.*

Geoffrey Gee, C.B.E., B.Sc., Sc.D., F.R.S.
*Professor of Chemistry and Pro Vice Chancellor, University of
Manchester until retirement in 1977.*

Andrew M. Hindmarsh, M.A., D.Phil.
*Studied zoology and then conducted research in the evolution of
animal behaviour at Oxford. Academic administrator in the
University of Sheffield. Methodist Local Preacher.*

Andrew Hunter, M.Sc., M.D., F.R.C.S., F.F.A.R.C.S.
Consultant Anaesthetist, Professor Emeritus, Department of Anaesthesia, Royal Infirmary Manchester; also Adviser on Organ Transplantation.

Ian Leck, M.B., Ch.B., Ph.D., D.Sc., F.R.C.P., F.F.C.M.
Professor of Community Medicine, University of Manchester. Methodist local preacher.

David Shaw, B.Sc.
Methodist minister and formerly a science teacher. Presently serving in Cheadle Hulme and Handforth.

Peter Summers, L.I.Biol., B.A.(Theol).
Methodist minister, formerly involved in genetics and fermentation technology. Presently serving in the Thetford circuit.

Norman Thorley, B.Sc., Ph.D., C.Phys., F.Inst.P.
Was Senior Lecturer in Physics, University of Newcastle upon Tyne. Lately Chief Scientific Adviser, Home Defence, Northern Region (Home Office).